Against the Odds

First published in 2013
by Londubh Books
18 Casimir Avenue, Harold's Cross, Dublin 6w, Ireland
www.londubh.ie
1 3 5 4 2
Origination by Londubh Books; cover by bluett
Printed by ScandBook AB, Falun, Sweden
ISBN: 978-1-907535-29-1

Against the Odds

Living with Motor Neurone Disease

Andy McGovern

LONDUBH BOOKS

Dedication

This book is dedicated to all my disabled friends and colleagues, who never cease to inspire me as they gain sight of new horizons by having the courage to leave the shores of the familiar.

The book is also specially dedicated to those people whose lives have been touched by motor neurone disease: to the many dear friends I have lost along the way – a little piece of my heart went with you as you lost your brave battle against the disease; to the three hundred and twenty people in Ireland today who live with MND – we are bonded together by the hope for a future cure; to those who tomorrow will hear the shocking words, 'You have motor neurone disease'– I would like you to take a little inspiration from my story.

MND may ravage your body but it can never reach your soul, your fighting spirit, or the love that fills your heart.

Acknowledgements

As I am a man with just a simple national school education from the 1930s and 1940s, the very idea of writing a book instilled fear in me. It would still be a remote, unreachable dream were it not for the help and support of some wonderful people. Their expertise and their generosity in sharing their knowledge ignited in me determination and the belief that all things are possible. With new-found confidence I took up the challenge of writing my life story. Míle buíochas to the late Deasún Breatnach, who shared with me so much of his time and wisdom throughout the years of our friendship, and to his son, Caoilte, who followed in his father's footsteps, giving me valuable advice and support.

Twelve years ago, I took part in a course sponsored by the Leitrim Association of People with Disabilities, coordinated by Sr Emmanuel Farrelly and funded by Leitrim County Partnership. Twenty participants completed the course and received introductory certificates from the National University of Ireland, Maynooth. The lecturers, instructors, teachers and participants on the course were a great help to me when it came to thinking positively, setting goals and asserting my rights. Thank you all.

Thanks to the Leitrim Development Company and CEO Tom Lavin for their generous sponsorship of these memoirs. Thanks to the Irish Motor Neurone Disease Association, which continues to support patients and strives to find a cure for this terminal disease and which lent me a computer and printer seventeen years ago. It is my privilege to support the association through the sales of this book.

I am grateful to the Central Remedial Clinic, Clontarf, and their assistive technology technician, Dr Ger Craddock, who provided me with computer training. My heartfelt thanks to CASA, the Caring and Sharing Association, for including me in their Lourdes pilgrimages and many other social events. I would also like to thank the Leitrim branch of the Irish Wheelchair Association, which never fails to help me in any way possible. I will always be deeply grateful to Nuala Tierney (now retired), Vivienne, Julie and the team at the National Rehabilitation Hospital, Dún Laoghaire, who achieved so much in restoring some independence to my life.

Thanks to Kathleen, my home help over twenty years, and my two weekend helpers, Rosemary and Mary. Heartfelt thanks to my daughter-in-law, Mary, who is my devoted carer 24/7. Thanks to my brother, Jack, who never fails to be there when needed. Thanks to my publisher, Jo Donoghue of Londubh Books, for all her guidance, expertise and support. Thanks to the friends who are part of the fabric of my life; it has been a pleasure to walk the road of life with you all.

I owe my deepest gratitude to Bridgie, my wife of fifty-two years, and our six wonderful children: Andrew, Raymond, Caroline, Anita, Sheila and Pauline. We have shared great times and together faced some tough challenges, which have cemented our family bond. My children, their spouses and my nine grandchildren are my treasures and my legacy. Their constant support is what sustains me. I love them all very much.

Contents

Foreword by Jimmy Magee
Patron of the Irish Motor Neurone Disease Association

My eldest son, Paul Magee, passed away from motor neurone disease in May 2008, at the age of fifty-one. His deterioration was rapid: in succession he lost the use of his arms, legs, feet, hands and voice, until, for the last five months of his life, he couldn't speak, couldn't shake his head, couldn't point a finger. The only thing he could do was smile. I will always remember him for his smile. If you told him a story he thought reasonably funny he would smile. If you asked him a question and the answer was, 'Yes,' he would smile. He had no way of communicating, 'No'.

It's not life's natural order to have your children predecease you. In Paul's case it was particularly difficult to understand because for his whole life he had been an enthusiastic sportsman, engaging in running, bowling, football and golf, all to a relatively high standard. This required dedication, strength and fitness, yet after a year and five months of living with MND, he was gone. During his time with the condition Paul and indeed the rest of our family had many questions. The Irish Motor Neurone Disease Association (IMNDA) became the first point of contact for a lot of these queries, as well as for practical and emotional support.

Paul's battle with this relentless disease showed us, his family and friends, the true meaning of the strength of the human spirit. The same quality, over a much longer period of time, is evident in every page of Andy McGovern's memoir, *Against the Odds*.

Paul knew there was no cure for motor neurone disease and that there certainly would not be one in his time. While he was still able to speak, he decided to bequeath his brain to Beaumont Hospital for MND research. I would love to see it playing a part in achieving a breakthrough for this terminal condition. For me, this would be the greatest legacy that any of my family could leave the world.

Like Paul, my father died prematurely and my wife Marie died at the age of fifty-four, but as Andy McGovern demonstrates time and again in *Against the Odds*, the best antidote to loss – whether the loss of loved ones or, in Andy's case, the loss of the use of his arms and hands that provided a living for his wife and six children – is what I call 'the glass half-full' attitude. Andy lists all the things he can do, not those he can't, when he writes: 'I can smile to brighten someone's day. I can laugh. I can think. I can write. I can read. I can drink Guinness through a straw – it tastes the same. I can enjoy fun. I can love. The list is endless.' And he has proven not once but twice that he can, with the help of technology, write a book.

Since I first met Andy, through the IMNDA, I have considered him an inspirational figure. In this book he attributes his strength of character to the example of his parents' generation. I don't know where he got his huge courage but it is an example to everyone, able-bodied or disabled.

My son Paul is with me night, noon and morning. I hope, for his sake and for the sake of all those who have been diagnosed with the condition and the extended MND community in Ireland, that we find that evasive cure and make real the vision of the IMNDA: 'Together, we will beat motor neurone disease.'

Introduction

At the age of forty-three I was on top of the world. I was married with a wife and six children, I had my own business and the world was mine. As I busily planned our future, I was not to know that the hand of fate was about to intervene and change everything. Our dreams came crashing down on us and all our hopes and aspirations lay shattered at our feet when I was diagnosed with motor neurone disease, a terminal illness of the central nervous system.

The story I now share with you is one of picking up the pieces and putting the jigsaw back together. It is a story of digging deep to find the inner hero and summoning every ounce of courage and strength that a human being can find. During the early years of this disease I experienced the daily struggles of living with a disability: frustration, anger and feelings of helplessness. Then slowly, like the phoenix from the ashes, I shook off my mantle of despair. I came to accept my disability, I reclaimed my life and, gradually, I found my rainbow's end. To my amazement, I once more tasted the joys of living.

My greatest desire is that my story will bring inspiration to other disabled people to have the courage to deal with their situation. All royalties from the sale of this book will go to the Irish Motor Neurone Disease Association (IMNDA), which supports those who suffer from this devastating disease and also those who search for a cure for it. A cure may not be found in my lifetime but that does not worry me. If I'm not here to witness it, I will smile from the heavens above, knowing that I have made a small contribution to this achievement.

As I approach my eightieth birthday, I look back on my own life. It has been a wonderful life, with all the emotions that any human being could expect to experience. I grew up in an era very different from today. I believe that no generation has seen as many changes as the people who were born in the 1920s, 1930s and 1940s. I know that we all live in periods of change but the changes that have taken place in Ireland over the past seventy years have taken everyone by surprise. I am fortunate to have witnessed this period. I write my story so that my children and grandchildren and future generations can know something about the Ireland of the past and the way of life of its great people.

When I look back over the past eight decades, my heart swells with pride that I was born into this now nearly forgotten era. I have received much inspiration from the brave people of the past who ploughed the fields and tilled the land with one purpose in mind: survival. My wish in writing this book is to create a permanent record of the people who by their resilience carved out my destiny. I wish to pay tribute and, in my own humble way, preserve their memory, as they made me who I am.

I know that some people will find it hard to identify with the kind of life I was born into. But I can assure my readers that I experienced much happiness growing up, with laughter and a neighbourly bond among people that seems almost foreign to us today. I am proud of my place of birth and also of my adopted parish, Cloone, the birthplace of my wife, children and grand-children, as well as my grandmother, Roseann O'Rourke of Sunnamore.

I was born in 1933 on a small farm in Corroneary, Aughavas, County Leitrim and educated at the local national school until I was thirteen. For a period, I worked on our farm, then I went to London in the early 1950s, where I worked in construction and bartending. I got married in 1961 and in 1964 my wife, Bridgie, and I returned to Leitrim, where we reared our six children and I had a machine contracting business. In 1977, I was diagnosed with motor neurone disease. Today, thirty-six years on, I am still alive, much to the amazement of my neurologists. As this is a progressive disease, I am now severely disabled and have lost almost all power in my hands and arms, but I am grateful for the abilities I still have.

I wrote this book with the help of modern assistive technology, in the form of Dragon NaturallySpeaking voice-recognition

The author at his computer, January 2012. (Photo: James Connolly, the Irish Independent*)*

software. The Irish Motor Neurone Disease Association lent me a computer and the software, which allows me to write by speaking into a microphone and on occasion using a foot mouse. The whole process demanded a lot of concentration but it was the only way for me to tell my story.

A disability can ignite initiative in a person and become the stepping stone for them to pursue other projects. This is the reason I'm writing the story of my life, as well as wishing to pay tribute to the inspiring people I met along the way.

Andy McGovern

SIGNATURE BY MOUTH

1

Earliest Memories

My earliest memory is like a dream of a most beautiful sound. I was standing in the doorway of our kitchen in Corroneary. On reflection, I realise I didn't know where I was at the time. A group of people had gathered on the flagstone outside our door and the sound that came from them captured my attention. Almost immediately my father approached the group and whatever he said to them made them turn and head away. I was very disappointed by this sudden departure but, being so young, I said nothing.

Many years later, I found the answer to the mystery of this dreamlike memory of 1935, when I was two years and almost eleven months old. It was Christmas and my grandmother (RIP) had died during the night. The group that arrived at our door the next morning, St Stephen's Day, were the wren boys or mummers. They did not know about the death in the house and when my father told them they said they were very sorry for the disturbance and left. I don't remember my grandmother – not her dying, the wake, the funeral or any of the traditional events that accompanied such a death. But that beautiful sound has lived on in me all these years.

As I grew up I was fascinated by this annual tradition – the wren boys arriving in colourful motley clothing with straw hats and lace curtains hiding their faces, carrying the little dead bird as a symbol of their celebration. They played céilí music and danced on the flagstones, then one of them rattled a tin can and asked for a donation, reciting the traditional lines:

> *The wren, the wren, the king of all birds,*
> *On St Stephen's Day was caught in the furze;*

Andy with his grandmother,
Roseann McGovern
(née O'Rourke), in 1933.

Up with the kettle and down with the pan,
Pray, give us a penny to bury the wran.

The story goes that the eagle invited all his feathered friends to take part in a competition to see who could fly the highest. The winner would then be declared 'king of all birds'. The eagle soared skywards, to a height no other bird could reach, leaving all the other birds far behind. By then he was exhausted and he decided to rest but, unbeknownst to him, the little wren had been hiding in his feathers all the time. The cheating wren emerged and flew higher and higher, thus becoming 'king of all birds'.

Another story has it that St Stephen, hunted by his enemies, was betrayed by the wren. The saint hid deep in the woods but the wren followed him and kept chirruping over him, leading his pursuers to him. Yet another story tells of Irish warriors being thwarted in their attempt to ambush a camp of Viking invaders in the middle of the night. A flock of wrens descended on the camp and started beating the drums with their beaks. The Vikings awoke, alerted to the imminent attack, and easily defeated the Irish.

The wren is a very handsome wee bird. Its nest is a work of art, as round as a ball and completely enclosed, apart from a little entrance. As a garsoon (Irish *garsún*), I was fascinated by the way the little bird could create such a structure, using nothing more than its beak. Though delicate in appearance, the nest is insulated and cemented on the inside to make it weatherproof.

On St Stephen's Day the wren boys came at intervals. They used the money they collected for a barn dance later on, buying tea, loaves and jam and maybe half a barrel of Guinness, depending on the finances. Music was supplied free of charge and there was even competition among musicians for the honour. These barn dances went on well into the spring, with each group of mummers trying the outdo the one before.

The first group of wren boys to arrive at our house every St Stephen's morning was the Drumloughlins, led by their captain, Mike Joe Clancy. Mike Joe presented the money box with a big smiling face but, fair play to him, he was happy with whatever he got. The Drumloughlins had a spree in Clancy's later on in the year. I remember being home from England many years later and I was present at one of these celebrations.

My memories are clear from about the time I was three or four. I spent most of the day out and about in the farmyard, playing with my brother Jack and my sister Rosaleen. We were comfortable, although our home was humble. We didn't know any other way of life: we were just equal to our neighbours: no electricity, no running water, no toilet, just a free-for-all out the back in a ditch filled with moss. Every Saturday night we would wash by the fireside in a galvanised tub, which was used on other occasions for washing clothes.

This was another chore for the women of the house: dirty clothes were put into the tub and, once the carbolic soap had been applied, the garments were scrubbed ferociously against a washboard with legs that stood on each side of the tub. Sometimes, when water in the immediate vicinity was scarce, the women carried the whole caboodle to the river, singing songs and scrubbing until the clothes were clean. Then they carried all the equipment back to the house, where the items were dried, ironed and starched.

In the evenings, a pot lid, or sometimes a brick, was warmed on the fire and placed in the bed, securely wrapped in an old newspaper or cloth. After a while it was moved to another bed. The windows and doors were far from airtight, and on a cold winter's night, you would hear the wind whistling through the house. The bitter cold meant that, without the heat from the pot lid, going to bed was not much warmer than going outside. Sometimes old coats were use as blankets but nobody complained.

There was a convenient item in the kitchen known as a settle bed. This timber structure, about six feet long, which opened and closed on hinges, provided sleeping accommodation for up to three children. The mattress was made of good clean straw and it was a treat to be told, 'You're sleeping in the settle bed tonight.' The sheets were made of sewn-together flour bags carrying the brand 'Heart's Delight'. Indeed it was our hearts' delight to get into that bed. I'm told that some thrifty, handy women were able to remove the logo from the flour bags by applying paraffin oil to the writing before making the bags into sheets. In the morning the bed was folded up to provide a worktop that looked really attractive in the kitchen.

Every night we went on bended knee to recite the Rosary: sorrowful, glorious or joyful mysteries, depending on the day of the week. The 'Hail, Holy Queen' and the litany of the Blessed Virgin followed but the real agonisers were the trimmings. Every family member who had passed away for two generations back was mentioned and then the animals and the neighbours' animals and, of course, the weather. The Rosary went on and on and if a child were caught laughing or giggling, they could be put outside the door for the remainder of the prayers. Family members knelt down with their backs to the fire and most were in their bare feet with heels to the blaze so the black soles of the feet were a common sight in the flickering flame. Sometimes a sibling pulled a twig or branch across the sole of your foot to make you laugh or shout, something that resulted in your being put outside. The Rosary was a great devotion, as well as providing priceless entertainment for the young ones.

With its large fireplace, the kitchen was the only place that had

The McGovern homestead, Corroneary, Aughavas, built in 1930 by stone mason Bernie McCabe.

any heat during the winter but as there was also a very big chimney and heat has a tendency to rise, most of the kitchen was not very warm. There was definitely no danger of carbon monoxide poisoning. I remember racing for the kitchen one cold morning with not a fledge of clothes on me. I wee-weed into the ashes at the corner of the fireplace but just as I was finishing, I noticed a strange man sitting at the table. Later I got to know him as Phil Charles. He had come to help my father wheel freshly-cut turf on the bog. All he said was, 'Drain it out, yeh boy, yeh!' I got such a fright that I went up the stairs two at a time. I didn't want to see this man again that day.

John Moran, a creamery manager from Mohill, boarded in our house. He came back for dinner every day at one o'clock and if I happened to be out on the street splashing in water holes John, who was a big man, would let out an enormous shout: 'Get into the house, ye little rascal, yeh.' I would run for my life to the stone that stabilised the crane in the corner of the fireplace and sit there until he finished his dinner and went back to work. Soon I got to know his time for dinner and I would make sure to be on that stone before he arrived. Many years later, when I returned from England, John had the welcome of the world for me but I could never warm to him. It just goes to show that one should never shout at a small child or a young dog.

We had food in abundance. There was plenty of cow's milk and we had a goat, the milk of which was supposed to be the best you could drink, although it had a wild taste of herbs. A pig killed in November supplied pork and bacon for several months. We also ate rabbits, which were lovely when roasted, and there were plenty of surplus cock chickens. We had all the vegetables we needed and lots of hen and duck eggs. We ate oatmeal porridge twice every day.

There was no such thing as buying meat from the butcher in town and I often wondered how these businesses survived. Sometimes if a farmer got a good price for an animal at the fair, he might buy a piece of mutton. The farmer, such as my own father, put this meat in the corner of the ass cart and if he had a few drinks, it might be well trampled before he got home. We children were on the lookout for this choice food and, before the ass was removed from the cart, the mutton was on the pan. My father then came into the kitchen, tired after his day's work and his few drinks and getting a good price for his animal. He soon fell asleep and was very lucky if there was any mutton left when he woke up.

Michael Gilmartin (wearing apron) and his father, Jimmy, blacksmiths in Mohill.
The customer is the owner of the horse, 'Baby Morris'. This photo was taken in the 1960s.
As Henry Wadsworth Longfellow wrote in 'The Village Blacksmith':

'He goes on Sunday to the church,
And sits among his boys;
He hears the parson pray and preach,
He hears his daughter's voice,
Singing in the village choir,
And it makes his heart rejoice.'

2

Life and Death

My mother, Mariah McGovern from Drumbad, Ballinamore, was born in 1894. She was one of a family of twelve, seven boys and five girls. She married my father, James McGovern of Corroneary, in 1927. Prior to her marriage, she worked as a milliner and seamstress in Hubert Reynolds's draper's shop in Ballinamore. There wasn't much demand for this skill when she arrived in Corroneary, although she did buy a new Singer sewing machine, a rare item in the district. She made our clothes and helped the neighbours out with Holy Communion, Confirmation and wedding outfits, all for no reward. Her main occupations were working on the farm, milking cows and feeding sows, digging the potatoes for the dinner, boiling the cabbage and getting the dinner to the bog on time. She also renovated the clothes that came in a parcel from America, reducing them to a usable size.

My mother was a very humble person with great love for her neighbours. When a couple with the same surname got married, they were believed to be blessed with home cures, especially for whooping cough. I remember several people coming to our home to ask my mother to make the cure for whooping cough. It consisted of prayers and some food cooked by the person with the cure: for example, a cake of oaten bread or, if the patient was a baby, some warm milk. The cure never failed but my mother could not take any payment for this inherited gift. The family who received the cure would be grateful and later that year a young girl or garsoon would be sent to help out with some chore, such as bringing in the hay. This was the way it was at that time: neighbours gave no payment for a day's work and none was expected.

My mother's only entertainment or leisure was the occasional visit home to Drumbad. She had a bicycle, another rare commodity in the 1920s, and she visited her two sisters who were married in Gorvagh, Mohill. She loved going to a draper's shop and she would arrive home in great humour after buying some cloth. This she stored for something the family or the house might need, such as curtains, or indeed any garment a neighbour might need. She would be ready for any emergency: a birth, death or marriage.

I don't think my mother ever had a holiday and she was never absent from home until the day of her funeral in 1977. She never visited a public house or dance hall in her married life but she was happy looking after the hens, turkeys, chickens, pigs, cows, calves and of course her three children and her husband, the love of her life. Large crowds attended her wake, removal and funeral Mass, when the neighbours paid their respects to this humble person who had been part of their everyday life for the previous fifty years. She never had much money, stylish clothes or modern conveniences but was always willing to share the little she had: a setting of eggs, a few bottles of milk, a bowl of sugar, half a cake of bread or maybe some bags she would patch for a neighbour's threshing. God be with her. When I think of her I remember the lines: 'Only the actions of the just//Smell sweet and blossom in their dust' from James Shirley's poem, 'Death the Leveller'.

The housewives and mothers of that time were the driving force behind the family. They were first up in the morning and last to bed at night. The final chore of the day was to lift the big pot of potatoes that were boiled for the pigs off the fire crook and leave it at the dresser. It was the menfolk who were in charge and the women did all their work silently, never dominating or dictating or demanding praise or recognition for their achievements. But without their wives some of the men were absolutely useless. At the dance in Maguire's hall, Francie Carroll would recommend: 'If anyone of you is looking for a good woman look for the track of the big black pot [the pig's pot] on her knee.'

If his wife was missing for half a day, a husband would die of the hunger, unable to make himself a simple cup of tea. When she returned home, she would have the sympathy of the world for him:

'The poor man nearly died with hunger while I was away.' Rose Morrow of Killevaha, Annamore, lived through that era and wrote about her life as a farmer's wife:

> *The farmer's wife has a busy life,*
> *She is rushed right off her feet,*
> *Feeding grunting sows and milking cows,*
> *Making butter fresh and sweet.*
>
> *She must bake the bread, cook the cabbage head,*
> *All the culinary arts display.*
> *In apple pies she must specialise,*
> *When it comes to saving hay.*
>
> *Hubby's underwear she must repair,*
> *And sew on buttons tight.*
> *She must wash his clothes and darn his hose.*
> *Have his collar snowy white.*
>
> *If he takes a chill, as he sometimes will,*
> *And declares he has the flu.*
> *She must understand and hold his hand,*
> *As a well-paid nurse might do.*
>
> *She must learn to soothe every pain and mood*
> *Of children big and small.*
> *Of vitamins count the exact amount*
> *That gives best results to all.*
>
> *If, by chance, they go to a dance,*
> *She must vie with the nicest there:*
> *Or he'd say, 'My sweet, your figure's not neat,*
> *Why don't you curl your hair?'*
>
> *Or, 'Your hands are rough,' he will say in a huff*
> *Such taunts cut like a knife.*

Yet all the while she must wear a smile,
The busy farmer's wife!

In my youth, nothing was thrown out and there was no such thing as rubbish. A refuse collector of that era would have died of hunger. A cardboard box was a gift and a tea chest was a resource for rearing children. You would have to put your name down and be popular with the grocer to get one. A child who was starting to crawl or walk was placed in the tea chest to keep it safe until it understood the dangers of the open fire. A bed of nice clean straw kept the chest dry and allowed the child to lie down. When the youngster was released from the tea chest, there was usually another child to take its place. One tea chest often reared a whole family.

Colds and flus were common and treated with home cures. The advice was: 'Feed a cold and starve a fever,' but in this lean period, I think both were starved. A great cure for respiratory illnesses was whey, produced by boiling milk and extracting the watery substance.

In 1918 what was called the 'Spanish' flu claimed many victims in our district. In one house five people died. Three corpses left the house on the same day and two followed a few months later. You can imagine the publicity this would cause today but, in those tough days, people accepted it as God's will. The headstone of the unfortunate family can still be viewed in the old graveyard in Aughavas, a memento of this terrible epidemic. One child survived and later emigrated to the US. His descendants returned to the parish on many occasions to see the headstone, revisit the landscape and think about the family's history. But for that child's survival and the grace of God, the Mulholland family would be no more.

Around this time a doctor was attending the families of farmers, many of whom had died from the flu. The story is told that the doctor came upon one family home where, to his surprise, everyone was healthy. When the doctor asked what the household was doing that was different, the wife replied that she had placed a cut-up onion in a dish to ward off infection. The sceptical doctor had one of the onions placed under a microscope and found it contained the flu virus. It had obviously absorbed the infection, thereby keeping the family safe from illness. The point of the story is that onions are a great remedy for infection.

I witnessed my mother doing the same thing with onions seventy years ago, to keep colds and flu away, and I heard a similar story from a business woman who placed several bowls of onions in her shop to ward off flu among her staff and customers. I have also heard that garlic is a powerful weapon in the fight against bacteria.

A boiled onion was a cure for earache and hot salt applied to the neck was a cure for tonsillitis. No doctor was ever called to treat colds or flu. They were just annual occurrences that would eventually go away and were believed to provide the body with resistance to other illnesses. The main worry was that everyone would be struck down with the flu at the same time and that there would be nobody to attend to the livestock or help out with sick family members. There were no phones or means of communication but neighbours always looked out for telltale signs, such as no smoke from a chimney at a certain time in the morning or no noise or movement in the farmyard. Either of these occurrences would surely prompt someone to investigate.

Such was the bond in the community that if a woman lost her husband through illness or an accident, the neighbours would turn out at full strength and the work of the farm, such as cutting the turf, saving the hay, harvesting the crops and digging the potatoes would be taken in hand by a *meitheal* (group of men). Much the same applied if a young wife died, leaving a husband and children. The neighbouring women would attend to the housework and take care of the children, while the menfolk continued with the *meitheal*, helping to ensuring that all farm work was completed satisfactorily.

When I was a child there were plenty of large families but if you investigate further, for example in the census returns from 1901, you will see that one or two children often died shortly after birth and there was no reference to the cause of death. It was imperative to have babies christened as soon as possible, as babies who died with original sin on their souls could not be buried in consecrated ground. Instead they were buried in a particular spot near their home or in a burial area also used by other families of the locality.

Folklore tells us that if a person accidentally stood on one of these infant graves at night they got disorientated and lost and it might be daylight before they discovered the gap out of the field. This was known as 'walking on the stray sod', something, people believed, that had originated with the fairies. But if you turned your coat inside out you would find the gap or gate.

When I was three or four I went out to the field with my father on a cold winter's day and as a result developed tonsillitis. I was in bed for a few days but I got worse. I don't remember this episode but I've heard it related many times. My neck and head swelled up and I was finding it hard to breathe. At three o'clock one morning my parents decided that the only way to save my life was to send for the doctor. My father went to Farrell Lee's, the nearest house to ours, and Peter Kilkenny, a farm hand, was sent on a bicycle to the doctor in Mohill, eight miles away. He rode as hard as he could and arrived at the doctor's house at four that morning. He knocked and finally the doctor appeared, not very pleased, and asked, 'What's up?'

The messenger replied, 'There's a child dying in Aughavas.' He gave the doctor the name and directions. The first question the doctor asked was: 'Is there any money out there?' Peter replied, 'I'm sure you will be paid.' The doctor wrote out a prescription and told Peter to get it filled in the chemist's when it opened at ten. He said he would go out to the sick child later on. Peter stayed in the town all morning with nothing to eat. At ten he went to the chemist and produced the prescription but there was a charge and he had no money. He had to go to an aunt of mine in the town to get money for the prescription. He also got tea and something to eat, then cycled home with the medicine. But I was too weak to take it.

At three in the afternoon the doctor arrived. He made no apologies for being so late, just asked where the sick child was. My mother directed him to the room. He closed the door and spent some time on his own with me. Then he came back to the kitchen with stethoscope around his neck and briefcase in hand. When my mother enquired, 'How is Andy?' the doctor took a deep breath and said, 'He'll be dead in an hour.' At that very moment a curate in our parish, Terry Meehan, entered the kitchen. His house adjoined our land and he was a frequent, casual visitor to our home. When he heard the doctor, he was furious and said, 'He won't die. I'll see to that.' The priest turned and walked out the door, followed by the doctor. He went straight to the church, a half-mile away, and said Mass. A priest was allowed to say only one Mass per day – he would have to get permission from the bishop to say another – but Father Terry knew there was no time to seek permission and was prepared to face the consequences of his decision.

The sun was sinking behind a drumlin in the parish of Aughavas that afternoon but the sun was rising in the face of a little boy in his home in Corroneary. My parents could not believe the miracle that was happening before their eyes. Each time my father entered the room he would ask me, 'How are you, Andy?' Each time the answer was the same: 'I'm all right.' Great promises were made. I would have to have my tonsils removed, so that I would not get an illness like this again. But the fact of the matter is that I never had my tonsils removed and I never got tonsillitis again. I never met Father Terry Meehan and I cannot recall anything about my sickness but I do know that I owe my life to this priest and I feel deeply indebted to him. I have prayed for him on many occasions. May God rest him.

Years later, when I was at home on holiday from England, I met Peter Kilkenny, the messenger to the doctor that day. An old man by then, he was delighted to be reacquainted with me and we went for a drink in the little village of Kesh. He recalled the night I was going to die, the hardship of riding a rattling bicycle to Mohill at all hours and the doctor enquiring, 'Is there any money out there?' Then he laughed heartily and said, 'Seeing you now, Andy, it was all worth it. It's your turn to buy; you owe me this one. It's payback time.' I gladly obliged.

When I was a child, death brought with it grief, loss and a sense of finality but wakes also included humour, laughter, singing and dancing. I was told that matchmaking was common and that some marriages were made at wakes. There was storytelling, and jokes were told about the deceased, especially if he or she had lived a good long life. Children were not welcome at wakes and when I was fourteen or fifteen and began to attend them, it was a sign that I was growing to be an adult. I remember looking forward to going to wakes in the 1940s and 1950s.

All clocks and timepieces were stopped at the moment of death and mirrors covered and turned to face the wall. Female neighbours usually laid out the body, clothing it in a habit or Sunday best clothes. If the deceased were male, a neighbouring man was asked to shave him, an honour bestowed on someone special. Pennies were placed on the eyelids to keep the eyes closed and a Bible or prayer book under the chin to keep the mouth shut. A crucifix was placed on the breast and Rosary beads entwined around the fingers. Candles were lit and the relatives were led in. In old times, this was the time for crying (keening or *caoineadh* in Irish), lamenting the dead.

The wake went on all night and the body was never left unattended. The first few hours after death were considered very important in case the deceased woke up. The window was left open for two or three hours, to let the spirit out, and, after a few more hours, the window was closed tight again to keep the spirit out. It was supposed to be very unlucky to stand between the window and the corpse.

When you arrived at a wake, the first thing you saw was a table laden with clay pipes filled with tobacco. It was customary to take a few pulls from a lit pipe of tobacco and older people would encourage us young people to do so. It was lovely at the start but after a few pulls, the room would start to spin around and the youngster would have to race outside to get sick. The idea behind presenting a young lad with a pipe full of this tobacco was that he might never smoke again. The older men knew how to smoke and took things gently, while the younger lads would take long draws. Trying to remove the pipe from one's mouth was another dangerous transaction, as the shank would stick to one's lip and take a bit of skin with it.

There was a saucer of snuff on the table, for women visitors to take a pinch and inhale. A bowl of snuff was placed on the chest of the deceased, in case of any movement that would indicate that the person was still alive. Gradually, the snuff would disappear, as people, especially women, came to say their goodbyes: hence the old saying, 'disappearing like snuff at a wake'.

At midnight the Rosary was recited, and a string of prayers after it by some of the religious women who did not know when to stop. The litany of all the saints echoed throughout the house and each person responded with, 'pray for us.' Indeed, some bored and hungry members of the audience would reply in a mutter: 'Make tay for us.'

When the prayers finally came to an end, it was time for refreshments. Close friends of the deceased were the first to be entertained, generally moving to the parlour for the food. Some alcohol was presented to the favourites and the sound of a cork being withdrawn from a bottle of Guinness was the tell-tale sign that someone in the room was being well taking care of. The less you were thought of by the family of the deceased, the longer you waited for your refreshments.

I remember being at one wake in our district, in the company of a few other young lads, when I was in my early teens. We sat up in the corpse house all night, pretending that it was our duty and that we were mourning the departure of the deceased. We were the last to be invited to the room to eat and by then we were absolutely starving. Neighbouring girls were attending to the table and we had them busy carrying bread to us. That's all we got: tea, bread, butter and jam. One lad in our company had a ferocious appetite and consumed an enormous amount of loaf bread; he had probably gone into the second loaf. A girl attending the table, who was a bit grand, came in with a pot of tea and asked, 'Anyone for tea?' Young Dominic replied in an equally posh accent, 'Yes, please, as a matter of fact I was more dry than hungry.' Well, trying to stop laughing in the church is hard but this was much worse. We were lucky that none of the family of the deceased was present, or we would surely have been run and our families would have been disgraced for sending brats like us to a wake.

The next day, the body was removed to the church. Four chairs were arranged outside in the street and the coffin was placed on them. After some more prayers, four strong men lifted the coffin and carried it shoulder high to the waiting hearse. The tradition was that the chairs were immediately knocked over; I don't know why.

The four men were close relatives of the deceased but if by any chance he or she had four sons, it was the greatest tribute that could be paid to any father or mother. The hearse was horse-drawn at this time and the procession consisted of horses and traps with some side cars, flanked by a large contingent of people on foot. The doors of the houses along the route were closed and all the curtains drawn and if anyone met the removal procession they turned around and walked with it for a distance.

On the day of the funeral the four strong men carried the coffin the longest way around to the graveyard. The grave diggers were neighbours and it was an honour to be chosen for this job. There was plenty of whiskey for the grave diggers and when all was completed, the shovels and spades were laid on the top of the closed grave in the form of a cross. Once the burial was over, a large number of neighbours headed for the public house, where there was more drinking and talking. If the deceased was not a young person, or had not died tragically, people would not mourn any longer. I heard a story about such a funeral, when even the widow got merry. The undertaker got into conversation with her and asked her to go out with him some night. She replied, 'I'm terribly sorry. You see, I promised to go out with that decent man who shaved poor Pat before he was laid out.'

There were two old codgers who drank together every weekend in the local pub. On their way home they had to pass by the graveyard where they would be buried one day. They made a promise that whichever one of them outlived the other would buy a miniature bottle of whiskey and sprinkle it on the other man's grave on his way home from the pub. Old Pat died and John, true to his promise, bought the bottle of whiskey. On his way home he went into the graveyard to visit Pat's resting place. He prayed for Pat, then he said, 'I've brought the little bottle of whiskey to sprinkle on your grave but I hope you don't mind if I run it through my kidneys first.'

3

Schooldays

I don't remember my first day at school, probably because I was always in the company of other children, primarily my own brother and sister. There was an older girl, Anna Rose Lyons, a neighbour, who called to our house on her way to school every morning. Anna Rose was like Mother Teresa to us, always helping with chores such as milking a cow or washing the creamery can or experimenting with some cooking. My mother adored her and so did the rest of us. She married Paddy Tummons and they had ten children and live in Enniskillen.

At school, my aunt, Mary Ford, was the infant teacher, so I suppose this made it easier for me. She lived with her husband, who was the principal teacher, not far from our house. There were four teachers in the school and an average of one hundred and twelve pupils. Mrs Ford never beat or chastised any child. That said, I got no special treatment from her. She encouraged children to start school young and even went to their homes so that they might get to know her and not be afraid to come to school. This, I believe, was in her own interest because if the average dropped, a teacher might lose his or her position and Mrs Ford would be the first to go, as she was less qualified than the other teachers. However, she was a very pleasant person.

Mrs Ford had no children herself but she embraced her pupils as if they were her own. She would warm their bottles of milk at the fire, ensure that each child had lunch, clean their little noses and faces and see to any other mishap to which the infants were vulnerable. She encouraged the children to wash their hands, especially the back of the hand – well, it's impossible to wash the back of the hand without washing the front of the other hand. This was a brainwave. Without a doubt she won the hearts of the little infants and their mothers.

The next schoolroom was occupied by first and second class and a teacher by the name of Miss McCabe was in charge. She was local but this did not make being in her class any easier. She taught us how to write, each letter reaching the top and bottom of the coloured lines in the copybook. It was woe to the pupil who took the pen in the left hand. She had big blue fists and I got many a wallop around the ear for misbehaving or not knowing something. It wasn't too severe, more like getting hit with a pound of butter. She also had a rod cut from the hedgerow and a few slaps from this was a lot worse than the big fist.

The next schoolroom was for third and fourth class. Here was another female teacher, Mrs Farrell. This one was a real terror, dressed smartly with dark hair tied back in a bun. She was married but her husband had left her, a rare stigma at this time. I firmly believe that she beat us just to relieve her frustrations. She had a son, Liam, attending the same school. He was the same age as me and a very likeable lad. We got on well together, sometimes too well, and got into mischief. She beat the hell out of her own son and, of course, I got it also. But we took our punishment as it was the norm and everyone was beaten at school. It toughened us for what was to come further down the line.

One morning I was at school earlier than usual. There was no one there except Mrs Farrell and Liam. She sent him on a message to a house about a half-mile away from the school and sent me to accompany him in case he was attacked by dogs. Well, as the two of us were good friends and working together, we had no fear of anything and we had a great time exploring everything we met on our way, including gates, gaps, watering holes and creamery cans.

On our way back to school after delivering the message, we came across a white sheet spread out on a whitethorn hedge. Something tempted us to throw a stone into the sheet and we kept doing this until the sheet disappeared down through the hedgerow. A dog barked then and we ran for our lives. It was a dastardly act – we were blackguards, little brats. When we arrived back at school we had long exceeded our estimated time and the teacher was furious. She beat us both black and blue but her own son got the worse beating. The other children watching were white-faced with terror. If she had known about the sheet I'm sure we would have been hospital material. However, it was a learning experience – I was never too early for school again.

I was by then approaching the age of eleven and the following September, I would be going into the master's room. He also beat the pupils. He was 6'2" and came from County Mayo. The female teachers often sent a misbehaving pupil into the principal's room to be chastised, a frightening thought, but I was prepared to go along with whatever would be. I was no better or worse than any of my classmates and it would be a relief to be finished with the other serpent of a teacher.

Any fears I had about going into the master's room were soon laid to rest as, on 4 February 1944, Master Ford had an accident. He was cycling home from Carrigallen on a Saturday night, going down a steep hill at high speed, when he lost control of the bicycle. He hit his head on the road and fell unconscious. He was taken home and the doctor attended him every day but he died four or five days later. He had suffered from high blood pressure for many years and I'm sure the few drinks he had that night contributed to the accident. He might have survived in the medical world of today but then there were no x-rays, brain scans or MRIs.

Mr Ford had owned one of the few motor cars in the districts, a Hillman Minx, but during the war years nobody except the emergency services could get petrol. When fuel came back on stream, the cars that were locked up in garages were of no use as their engines had seized up from want of running. As the proverb says, 'If you don't use it, you lose it.'

Corduff national school got a new principal teacher, Master Lynch, the following September. Again he was a man from the west of Ireland. He always wore a Donegal tweed suit with leather buttons and heavy boots with homespun woollen socks. He was small in stature with a purple face and double chin. He spoke a lot of Irish and preferred to use Irish rather than English for most of his teaching. We soon found out that he was very fond of the drink and cigarettes. He smoked continuously and on Monday mornings pupils would be on their best behaviour as this was no time for mischief. He would get into a rage at the least thing.

One morning the master was frantic for a smoke and he asked the children if any of them knew where he might buy some cigarettes. This was in the war years and cigarettes were very scarce. One pupil put his hand up and said, 'Please, sir, there are cigarettes in Bamey's [McKiernan's] of Drumreilly.' Drumreilly was about eight miles away and this pupil thought he would get the job of going for the cigarettes. However, the master beckoned me: 'Mac Samhrain [Irish for McGovern], go to Bamey's and get me some cigarettes and a box of matches.' He gave me some money and his bicycle. I had to ride the bicycle under the bar as I was not big enough to sit on the saddle and I didn't even know where Bamey's was. So I set off in the direction of Drumreilly. It took me some time to get there, travelling slowly.

Finally, after seeking directions from many people I met on the way, I arrived at the little shop. I presented my case and told the shopkeeper who had sent me. After some time he produced a packet of ten Woodbine. He took five cigarettes out of the packet and gave me the rest, taking the money. He also gave me a box of matches. I bought a twopenny packet of biscuits (Thin Arrowroot) for myself, regardless of the consequences. I started back, delighted with my purchase. I took it very easy – as a matter of fact I dilly-dallied all the way. The few biscuits kept body and soul together. All I had to keep in mind was to get back to the school before three o'clock, going home time.

I came around the final bend at a ferocious speed, still riding underneath the crossbar. Master Lynch was standing on the road in his Donegal tweed outfit and with the countenance of the devil. He shouted to me from a distance, 'Did you get the cigarettes?' I nodded. 'Give them to me and get into school.' I gave him the five Woodbine, the matches and his change. He never looked at the change, so the twopence for the biscuits were not missed. As I left his bicycle up against the wall, I observed him taking the first draw from the Woodbine. I thought that when he exhaled, the smoke came out his ears as well.

Master Lynch beat children for any little mistake, depending on the effects of his social life the previous night. He was small and could not get a right delivery of the rod on our hands, so he decided to get up on the chair for better delivery. Later on he replaced the rod with a leather strap about two feet long, one-and-a-half inches wide and a quarter-inch thick. It was tapered at one end to make it comfortable for the user's hand. Some said that he got it from the Christian Brothers' school, as the Christian Brothers had a reputation at the time for specialising in beatings.

Everyone wondered who would be the first to get this punishment and I hadn't too long to wait to find out. I was playing hurley one Sunday afternoon with my brother Jack. Neither of us was very skilled at this game. Jack took a swing at the ball and missed, making contact with my forehead and eye. For a while, I was completely blind in one eye and had a good gash over my eyebrow. But there was no word about going to the doctor. This was before medical cards were available and nobody went to the doctor except for serious illnesses.

On the following Monday morning I started out for school, my eye weak and running water. In class, we were to spend the lesson reading aloud together. The master chose me to read a page. I stumbled through it and he became enraged. I explained that my eye was watering but it made no difference to him. He shouted at me to read it again but I was even worse than before. He beckoned me up to the table and reached for the strap. This time he got up on the chair and climbed on to the table to give himself more elevation. He told me to hold up my hand and he gave me four of his best on each hand. My arm just dropped after each delivery, numb from the pain and the weight of the strap. When the punishment was over, I went back to my seat, very hurt.

At eleven o'clock the whistle went for a toilet break. The other children gathered around me, fearful but supportive. Some of them asked, 'What are you going to do?' I said, 'I'm not going in there any more today.' I jumped the four-foot wall that surrounded the toilets and took to the hills. At some stage I had to change my route and cross the road that led to the school, so I waited patiently, peeping out cautiously from time to time. I saw the tyrant out on the road looking for me but I was determined that he would not find me.

I waited until he returned to the school, then made a dash across the road and into the fields, like a frightened animal, using the hedgerows as shelter. Soon I arrived at a lovely glen at least thirty foot deep. The water was flowing down the rocks, making a beautiful sound and creating a lot of white froth. The sides of the glen were planted with pine trees, making it an ideal haven for a fugitive. I chose a nice dry rock and sat there listening to the sound of the water, my heart, which had earlier thumped so loudly with panic and fear, now at peace in this beautiful spot. The feeling of peace slowly filled my little body. My eyes were drawn to a lovely brown trout and I noticed the splendid colours on his back. I became one with that trout, free from fear and oppression, born free to enjoy nature's splendours at their best. So often, in my adult years, my mind travelled back to this magical moment of my youth.

While I sat in that glen, the teacher sent my brother Jack home to fetch me back to school, only for him to find that I was not there. My parents were furious when they heard what had happened. My father said not to worry, that I would come home when I was ready. Neither of my parents ever hit me in my life, nor any of my siblings. They might shout at us but that was all. Jack had to report back to the master that I had not gone home, something that worried him.

The next morning I was a bit fearful about going to school but my father said, 'Don't worry, Andy, he's not going to touch you any more.' I don't know what happened between parents and teacher but I do know the master did not say a word to me the next day or during the remainder of my years in school. The strap had disappeared. Later I was told that my good friend Liam Farrell had disposed of it down a small hole in the floorboards of the classroom and the teacher hadn't enquired what happened to it. My parents never said a word about my leaving school and I was a hero to my classmates and friends.

I hated that teacher for years but I discovered that hate only destroys the possessor. 'A person is only free when they get rid of hate and grudge.' I heard this said by John B. Keane years later, when he was interviewed on radio. According to Keane, 'A person holding a grudge is like a horse going into a race carrying unnecessary weight.'

My schooldays were enjoyable for the most part and I still love meeting up with some of my old classmates – Jimmy Hanrahan, Bernie McDermott, James McGovern, Pat McGuirl, Francie McIntyre, Sean Monaghan, Vincent Kenny and my brother Jack. We recall our time in school with great jokes and laughter.

Every year in April, we removed our shoes on our way home from school. This was a joyous event. Our parents never had to tell us to do it, nor did they disapprove. The shoes were not seen again until September. It was our first introduction to the summer that would follow. We felt so good that we thought we could run a hare. But accidents and discomforts followed. All the byroads at this time had rough surfaces and two-inch stones filled the potholes. This resulted in cut feet and stone bruises but these incidents were soon dismissed as minor inconveniences. There were other casualties caused by thorns, which caused a lot of pain when someone tried to extract them from the foot but there were home remedies, such as bacon fat applied tightly to the foot under a bandage. When the bandage was removed after about three days, the thorn would appear in the fat. Yes, it always worked.

As a child, I served Mass for many years and no priest ever abused or interfered with me. Sex was something you never heard discussed and I was very innocent and gullible regarding this taboo subject. I believe that we should have received sex education from our superiors in a gentle, informative manner. Children should not be exposed to sex by older, bragging, males who describe it as an animal act.

If I got a clip on the ear for misbehaving I deserved it. I was full of villainy. Our home was not far from the church and that meant one thing: I was always on call. My job was to serve Mass if some other server failed to turn up, usually in the winter time. I had to be in the church for eight o'clock Mass every morning and to get there

I had to pass through an old graveyard. Some mornings were so dark that the sound of a bird fluttering in a bush was enough to make the hair stand up on my head. At this time, many people believed in ghosts: they regularly told ghost stories around the hearth and prayers were said after Mass to banish the spirits who wandered through the world for the ruin of souls. We children were in bed when ghost stories were told, but, unknown to the adults, we were awake and listening. As a result, we were terrified to go out on a dark night.

Entering the church was no better than the graveyard. The church was empty and in darkness when I arrived, as this was the pre-electricity era. After a while, I'd hear a sound and see a dark figure in the distance. It was an old woman, Anne Blueman, whose job it was to ring the bell for Mass. But she was not allowed to serve Mass as no woman was allowed inside the altar rails, for what reason I do not know.

A big, strong man called John Shan lived in the parish. He was 6'4" or 6'5" tall and he depended on his physique for everything he did. Nobody could match him at any of the farm tasks, especially mowing with the scythe. One morning he was at Mass in Aughavas. The server failed to turn up and as there were only a few women in the church, the priest beckoned to John to come up and serve Mass. John did not know any of the Latin answers but was prepared to help the priest in whatever way he could.

The priest sent John to fetch the wine and water and utensils for him to wash his hands and John proceeded to the table that held the selection of cruets. He got confused and did not know which one to bring up to the priest. The table top was a marble slab about four inches thick and the table was never moved because of its weight. But John simply picked the table up in his massive muscular arms and proceeded to the waiting priest. In a loud voice, he said, 'There you are, help yourself.' When the priest finished taking the relevant material. John was still holding up the table. The priest signalled to him and he took the table back to its usual place.

Thank God, things have changed: women are now allowed on to the altar and participate in the services.

I remember my first Sunday serving Mass. My brother Jack and Pat Downey were the senior servers. At that time the priest had his back to the congregation and every time he genuflected, two servers would have to go and hold out his vestments, while the third rang the bell. Pat Downey knew that I had never been on the altar before, so it was my job to ring the bell. The striking implement had a soft padded ball on one end and a brass knob on the other. As Downey was on his way up with Jack to hold out the priest's vestments, he whispered to me, 'Hold the soft end in your hand. Otherwise it will hurt you.' When the priest genuflected and everything had been completed gracefully, it was my job to hit the bell. I hit it such a wallop with the brass knob that everyone in the congregation got a terrible fright and the priest must have jumped two feet in the air. Soon peace was restored, however, and the next time I hit the bell, it was with the soft end. After Mass the priest asked why I had hit the bell so hard. I replied that it was my first time serving Mass and that I had got confused. I did not tell him that Downey had tricked me. Pat Downey was a nice lad. He was full of villainy and mischief but you had to like him. It was a lesson in growing up for me; I certainly never trusted Downey again. This bell is serving the same purpose in Aughavas church seventy years on.

Another example of Downey's villainy involved a big young lad called Mike Baxter, who was learning to serve Mass. He never took part in any of the chores, just observed. Our parish priest, Pat O'Reilly, was very strict: all the Mass servers had to wear canvas slippers and not make a sound while on the altar, except for the appropriate Latin responses. We all dressed at the back of the altar. On this particular Sunday, Mass was over and Mike was down on one knee trying to loosen a hard knot on his slipper. Pat Downey was clearing some of the utensils from the altar. His job was to remove the candles and extinguish them and, as he was passing by Mike Baxter, Downey put the hot end of the candle to Baxter's neck. He let out such a roar that it could have woken the dead but Downey had gone out the other side and was bringing in the Mass book by the time Father O'Reilly arrived. Baxter was still holding his neck and shouting. Father O'Reilly thumped him for making such a noise in God's house and Downey got away with it, yet again.

With Confirmation on the way we had to go to the church on occasion for Father O'Reilly to give us instruction. One day we were in the church before the priest arrived. There was a pulpit near the middle of the church from which priests gave sermons. Again Pat Downey had a brainwave: he would lecture to us from the pulpit. Just when he was in full flow, the sacristy door opened. Downey had no time to make his escape; all he could do was lie down in the pulpit in the hope that he wouldn't be seen. Luckily for him, Father O'Reilly did not miss him from the class but the rest of us were on the verge of bursting out laughing. This would have given the game away and we would probably all have been chastised. Downey had to stay in the pulpit until the priest's class ended, long after everyone had left the church.

On another occasion, Father O'Reilly summoned us on our way home from school to collect surplices and take them home for our mothers to wash. Everyone got a surplice but Downey accidentally got a priest's surplice. He put on the big priest's surplice and told the rest of us to put on the ones we were carrying. Then he suggested that we would have a mock funeral. He went out in front – he was the leader – with the rest of us making up the parade. Downey was shouting out Latin phrases and we started answering him in Latin as well: '*Mea culpa. mea culpa.*' We entered the old graveyard and people could see this unannounced funeral from a distance.

Our display was short-lived. Father O'Reilly missed his surplice and followed us. He was absolutely furious when he saw the display in the graveyard and we ran for our lives with Father O'Reilly in hot pursuit. There was rough terrain with stones sticking up and we spread out so he didn't know which path to follow. We got the garments off, Downey hung his on a headstone and we made our escape. Father O'Reilly got his surplice back and the rest of us brought ours home to be washed. We expected Father O'Reilly to come to the school the next day and have us chastised but there was never a word about the incident. He probably saw the funny side to it.

4

Christmas

My memories of Christmas in the 1940s are very special. Preparations for this festival began in November. The first commodity that had to be got was fresh lime. Limestone came from a quarry and was brought to a limekiln where a fire was lit under the stones. With a hammer the stones were broken into fragments of about four inches in circumference and these were burned until they disintegrated into a white powder.

In earlier times, nearly every farmer had his own limekiln as it was essential to provide lime to fertilise the land. But lime was also in great demand for whitewashing. When added to sand, it produced mortar for building. It was hard work keeping limekilns going with very little reward and quite a lot in the district had closed down. But there was a renowned limekiln still producing best-quality lime at Castlefore, Fenagh. One year, my father decided that I should go there and get some lime to make whitewash for Christmas.

I started out with the horse and cart at nine o'clock on a Saturday morning to travel the nine miles to Castlefore. I was about fourteen but I had plenty of experience in working the horse and I appreciated the confidence my father placed in me by entrusting me with this manlike responsibility. I brought with me two bags of hay, one for the horse and one for me to sit on, as well as a bottle of fresh cow's milk and a few cuts of soda bread. My father told me that the road was flat and that there were no hills to cross. He also told me to get six hand boxes of lime, which was equal to three barrels, the amount he required.

I turned right at McCabe's shop and continued for six straight miles to Fenagh village. There I turned left out the Castlefore Road and was told to turn right two miles out that road, cross over an iron bridge and that the limekiln was only a few hundred yards from there. Up to this, I had negotiated everything successfully but the iron wheels of the cart made a terrible noise on the bridge and the horse became nervous. I had to restrain him with all my strength, all the while talking to him, saying, 'Take it easy, boy.' Fortunately he responded when I patted him on the rump to calm him down and we made our way safely across the bridge.

There were two big, strong men working at the limekiln. When I told them what I wanted, one of them asked where I came from and they laughed when I said, 'Aughavas'. 'You came all that way for lime?' one of them asked. 'I was told that ye had good lime,' I replied. He said, 'You will have to wait half an hour as we don't have the supply you want ready yet. But you can rest your horse.'

I took out the bag of hay and gave some to the horse. Meanwhile, I started on the bottle of fresh milk and the soda bread. I sat down beside the horse and we both ate, contented. There was no one within earshot and I found myself talking to the horse. I was sitting close to his head and I knew that he was responding to my speech. It's easy to know by a horse's eye and face if it is happy with you. At that moment, I think that we both knew that we were depending on each other for the success of this adventure.

One of the men eventually shouted at me to bring over the horse and cart. Soon they were loading me up with a box measure of the steaming lime. He said, 'That will have to do you, we are short. It will be well into the afternoon before we have more lime burned and that would mean you would be travelling home at night.'

I gave him the money and he gave me back the change. Then he went to his own pocket and gave me two shillings. He said, 'You are a good garsoon and you have a good horse but be careful, it's a long way from here to Aughavas. Go into Freddie Quinn's shop on your way home and get yourself a bottle of lemonade and some cakes.'

I thanked him and left. It was great to be recognised by these two strange, strong workmen. On the way back, I kept a firm rein on the horse and he negotiated the iron bridge with no fear whatsoever. I made myself comfortable, sitting on the bag of hay on top of the lime. At times I found my backside getting warm with the heat of the freshly burned lime and I wondered if it would ever start a fire in the cart. But I consoled myself with the thought that these two honest men would never have sent me out on a dangerous mission.

At Freddie Quinn's I moved on to the Cloone Road and pulled into the side. I got some more hay out for the horse. I went into the shop and got lemonade and cakes, then I sat down and watched the animal eat and, of course, I talked to him as if he were a human. I enjoyed the gift of the lemonade and cakes, Soon we were on our way, both happy with our steaming cargo. Further up the road, the horse gave a few fast steps and as we went on I realised that he had sensed a watering hole from a distance. At this time there were plenty of these drinking pools along every road for cattle and horses.

I reached home at five in the evening, when it was still daylight. I secured the hot lime in a shed to protect it from rain, stabled the horse and gave him plenty of hay and water. I twisted some hay firmly in my hand and gave the animal a brush down with it, bragging about him. I felt proud of that day's adventure.

The next day presented a different chore as it was time for the whitewashing to begin. It was very important to use the lime fresh, while it was still warm and alive. When water was added, the lime fizzed and fermented easily and became a white paste. The kitchen was tackled first but before that, every piece of furniture and all the utensils had to be moved to the centre of the kitchen floor, out of harm's way.

The whitewash was applied with a special brush that was used for indoor work only and was well protected in between the times of whitewashing. Another brush, known as a besom, was used for outdoor work on walls, piers and outhouses. It was hand-made of heather, which was evenly clipped at the end and wrapped tightly to a handle. When the whitewashing was done, the house walls and out-offices looked wonderful. The kitchen smelled fresh and had an echo. The smell of lime was a great fumigator and, when it reached into the other apartments of the house, insects such as cockroaches, crickets, moths, flies, spiders and many more unwanted creatures vacated the home for an outdoor shelter. Some didn't make it and were found dead on the floor the next morning. My mother filled a large container of spring water and added a small nodule of lime. She instructed us all to take a glass of this water in the morning, saying. 'That will kill any worms in you.' She was probably right and we did survive.

Turkeys were sold before Christmas, providing much-needed money for Christmas and well into the New Year. The rearing of a flock of turkeys involved little expense, except for food that was in the home, such as potatoes, oatmeal and oats. We also fed the turkeys chopped-up nettles. It was a common sight to see a flock of turkeys in a field where oats had been harvested. They could eat up any grain that escaped during the harvesting as well as some necessary herbs. A youngster would be sent with the flock to protect them from foxes and other predators.

The selling of the turkeys was something that was talked about for a long time before it happened. The prices paid by various buyers would be discussed. We always sold our turkeys to a fowl buyer named McGee, from Ballyconnell, County Cavan. He passed by our house every Wednesday of the year, buying eggs, fowl, rabbits, kid goats and blackberries when they were in season. He weighed every turkey with a small scales hanging from the back of his truck. The engine of the lorry was always running and vibrating, to whose advantage I do not know. He would then combine the weights of the turkeys, giving so much a pound for the entire lot. This would take some time as it was the pre-calculator era.

Some of the local women were not too happy with McGee's method, especially because of the vibration in the scales. My mother had a sister, Katie, married in Gorvagh. She kept plenty of turkeys and always sold them to a local fowl buyer, Sean Murphy. Her son Mike worked in Murphy's as a turkey plucker and she advised my mother to bring her turkeys to Murphy's.

On a cold Monday morning in December I was dispatched on the eight-mile trip with horse and cart. My mother followed on a bicycle. We had about twenty turkeys, hens and cocks, to sell. When we reached Murphy's I was directed into a yard and the helpful staff soon had all the fowl loaded into one container on a weighbridge. A man took one look at the scales and handed my mother a docket, saying, 'Go into the shop and collect your money.' My mother emerged smiling from the shop. It was obvious that the money she had got far exceeded her expectations. She bought some groceries and plenty of sweets and biscuits for me. She then said we were going to visit my aunt Katie – her sister – just a half-mile further on. I followed obediently. There was the welcome of the world for us in this house. My aunt Katie was also my godmother and she was delighted to see me now, transformed into a young man. I stabled the horse and gave him hay, water and oats, then went into the house where a big dinner awaited me.

The two sisters talked and talked as if they had never seen other before, totally oblivious of my presence, but soon it was time for me to tackle the horse and be on my way. I found the horse in great humour, mad to get home. It's amazing how animals can sense the atmosphere from people around them. For the first few miles, I had to pull hard against the horse before he settled to a comfortable walk. I had the sweets and biscuits to make the journey rewarding. My mother caught up with us and walked a portion of the way behind the cart. Then she said, 'I'll go on now and have a feed ready for you.' But I knew that she wanted to get home before me to share the excitement that was burning deep within her about the amount of money she got for her turkeys.

James Heslin, a blacksmith who lived at Corriga, reared a few turkeys one year. He was not married at the time and lived on his own. All the turkeys then were black or bronze; no such thing as a white turkey. James tended these turkeys very well and looked forward to making a few handy pounds for Christmas. A few weeks before Christmas, he presented the turkeys for sale to McGee, the fowl buyer who passed by his forge every Wednesday. McGee offered him three shillings and sixpence a pound for his turkeys but they had made three shillings and ninepence a pound in Arva the previous Friday. 'That's all right,' says McGee, and drove off. The following Friday James took his turkeys to Arva but all he could get for them was three shillings and threepence a pound. So he took them home and made up his mind that he would sell them to McGee the following Wednesday.

McGee arrived and James said, 'You can have my turkeys at last week's price.'

'Hold on now,' said McGee. 'Turkey prices are falling and all I can give you is three shillings a pound. James was furious. McGee said, 'You may give them to me. It's my last day on this route before Christmas.' But James said no way. McGee shouted, 'For the last time, give them to me.' James looked him straight in the eye and said, 'I'll hold the fuckers until they go grey in the head.' Later he sold his turkeys to the neighbours, at what price I do not know.

As part of the traditional Christmas preparations, my brother and I would go to Drumhallan hill in search of berried holly. We went at least two weeks before Christmas as the holly bush would lose most of its berries in the last few days before Christmas. I never could work out whether it was birds that ate the berries or people collecting this sought-after Christmas decoration. We secured ours and stored it in the barn. There it would hold its appearance and texture, unvisited by birds, humans or wind storms. The holly was a symbol of life. While other trees turned brown and looked dead, the holly bush had an abundance of wonderful greenery and berries, an indication that spring was just around the corner.

The whole house was decorated with holly: the window sashes, over the fireplace, the picture of the Sacred Heart, the dresser, the rack on the wall that displayed the glittering gallon lids. We used no artificial decorations and none were needed. The kitchen had the greenness of a tree and in the background the whitewashed walls sparkled. It was a welcoming display and everyone in the family was in good humour and happy to be able to celebrate another Christmas.

The morning of Christmas Eve was a busy day in our area, as well as being a very hungry day. Breakfast consisted of porridge, a boiled egg and some home-made bread. After breakfast, our parents would go to do the shopping, sometimes with the ass and cart. Items that had not been purchased since last Christmas would be included in the list: currants, raisins, semolina, rice, tea and sugar, salt, a bag of Heart's Delight flour, a few bottles of stout and a bottle of port wine. The grocer would also give a present – maybe a half-bottle of Jameson whiskey. By afternoon, our parents would arrive home with this cargo. My father might have consumed a few bottles of stout and we would all know it. We would be hiding our laughter at the mistakes he made – but looking back, I can say that he was never contrary or aggressive with drink. The dinner would consist of plenty of potatoes and home-made butter (a combination known as 'bruise'), washed down with a mug of fresh cow's milk. The meal was completed with tea and soda bread.

After dinner, the preparations for the Christmas dinner began. The meat could be a turkey, a goose, a pig's head, a duck or maybe two cock chickens, depending on what was surplus in the farmyard. In our house it was generally a turkey. It was killed and plucked and all the internals removed, then hung for about three days, probably from the beam in the hay shed. The head, neck and feet were cut off and my mother stuffed the turkey with her own recipe (even the craw was stuffed) and slices of home-cured bacon were placed on top of this massive bird. All was then lifted gently into the big metal pot, erected on an iron tripod about five inches high. Burning turf coals were placed under the pot and more added to the lid. Building up this furnace of coals was repeated many times, as the cooking of the turkey would take hours and go on well into the morning.

There was another traditional commitment that had to be fulfilled by all the family: Confession. My father would stay back to protect the house from any fire and attend to keeping coals to the big pot, then go to Confession himself when some of us arrived home. The house was glowing by then, with a candle lit in every window, each standing in a jam pot for protection against fire. By now the aroma coming from the cooking turkey reached out into the street. That delicious smell is something that will live with me for ever. The thought of having to wait until the following afternoon to taste it was sheer agony.

By the time we got home, our hunger was unbearable. However, we were given humble mugs of stirabout (porridge) and milk and sent straight to bed. My father would go out at midnight to attend to the cattle and give them an extra portion of hay to celebrate the festival. The dogs and cats would have plenty from the turkey's innards. Folklore had it that the ass would lie down and tumble at midnight on Christmas Eve in memory of the birth of Jesus. This animal was the only transport available to carry Jesus and his mother, Mary, from Bethlehem into Egypt. I've heard of some who tested this fable by bringing the ass into the kitchen at midnight but the animal refused to lie down. Probably the smell of the turkey was a deterrent.

On Christmas morning everyone was up early. The smell of the turkey in every corner of the house was agonising but we were not allowed to eat anything until we returned from Mass. You had to fast from midnight before receiving Holy Communion. We were lucky that we had to walk only a half-mile to the church; other people would have to travel three miles or more. When the priest was reading the gospel, everyone would stand up and before long you would hear bangs, as members of the congregation fainted from hunger and had to be carried out of the church. This requirement has been removed so there is no fainting in the church any longer.

After Mass it was a rush to get home for breakfast. On Christmas morning, the breakfast was special, as we had boxty. This food, made from potatoes, took three forms: pan boxty, boiled boxty (dumplings) and boxty loaf (baked in the oven like a cake). Our boxty loaf, cooked from the previous day, was sliced and fried on the pan until a golden brown. With it we would have a few slices of home-cured bacon. The aroma that filled the kitchen surpassed even the cooked turkey.

With full and plenty for breakfast, it was easy to wait for the Christmas dinner. At three o'clock, we all sat down at the table together for this long-awaited meal, all delicious home-produced food: beautiful flowery Champion potatoes and a selection of vegetables, washed down with mugs of milk. The sweet was plum pudding or semolina with strawberry jam and then tea with Christmas cake or currant brack. When we went outside after dinner, we could tell what the neighbours had eaten – turkey, duck or chicken – because, although the nearest house was some fields away, each dinner produced its own pleasant aroma that filled the air.

I often watch the professional cooks of today such as Kevin

Marcella Conboy of Aughavas with her four children and flock of free-range chickens.

Dundon, Rachel Allen and Neven Maguire, display their skills with mouthwatering presentations. They are lucky that radio and TV save them from having to convey the aromas of the food they cook. You can see and hear but you cannot smell. Nowadays we cook with fancy ingredients and spices to make dishes taste good but our food lacks the aroma and taste of those bygone days. Today's professional chefs are too young to have experienced the taste and smell that were released from the humble iron pot of the 1940s.

I will never forget the contentment and security of the Christmases of my youth. When Santa was no more for me I did get a pair of socks and a pullover, probably hand-me-downs. When the festive season was over, there would not be a five-pound note left in the townland but happiness, peace and pride remained in the hearts of these humble people.

5

The Farm

The majority of Leitrim farms had between five and thirty acres and all small farmers practised mixed farming, keeping a few cows, pigs, poultry, an ass and maybe a horse. A horse was considered a luxury. The principal work on the farm was growing potatoes and grain to feed the family and animals. The calves were sold on at the local cattle fairs in Mohill, Cloone or Carrigallen.

In the 1930s and 1940s people had very little in monetary terms but at a deeper level they had a great deal. There was a wonderful richness within the family because each family member was treasured and his or her contribution to the work of the farm was a vital link in the chain that ensured the family's survival. Young and old shared the daily chores of carrying water from the well, milking goat or cow, collecting eggs and gathering firewood, so everybody enjoyed a great feeling of camaraderie. We worked hard but many hands make light work. Each season brought its own responsibilities: hay and turf to be saved, crops to be set or harvested. We expected neither payment nor thanks: it was our duty and we did it with a light heart.

In the spring we prepared about an acre of ground for potatoes. First of all the ridges were marked out: this was known as 'cutting the lea' and was done with a horse and plough. Then it was time to prepare the ridge, also known as 'coping'. Three men worked with two horses: one man driving them, the second controlling the plough and the third tramping the turned-over sod. When this task was completed, the furrow was ploughed and earth supplied for the centre of the ridge. This was known as 'heartening' and was done manually with a spade or shovel. With an ass and creel we brought out cow manure and spread it on each marked-out ridge.

With the ridge was completed, it was time to plant the seed potatoes. Potatoes chosen for the purpose were brought into the kitchen, where sometimes a not very mobile older person would sit and cut the potatoes into portions known as 'splits', each one containing an eye. The portions of potato without an eye were discarded and boiled at a later stage for the pigs or hens. Two or three people would work in the field with a 'steeveen' (dibber), a home-made tool about four feet long with a peg nine inches from the pointed end. When you applied your foot to this peg, a hole was made in the ridge for the split or seed. A child would insert the seed into the hole; this was known as 'guggering'. In the afternoon, these holes were closed securely with the steeveen to protect the splits from crows or other invaders. After the potatoes were planted, the furrow was ploughed again manually and more earth applied to the ridge. This was known as 'shovelling' or remoulding, and it was said that the more the seedlings were 'interrupted' in this way, the better the new potatoes would develop under the heavy sod.

When the stalks appeared they were sprayed with bluestone and washing soda to protect the potatoes from blight; this process was repeated every three weeks until the end of August. In September the potato stalks died back and withered and the following month the crop was ready for digging. The workmen were good at their job: digging the potatoes with spades, throwing them on to the ridge and lining them up as if they were apples so that not one potato was damaged. It was then time for the children's chore. As soon as we got home from school, we were rushed to the potato field to pick the crop. The potatoes were stored in a pit or heap and covered with straw and earth to protect them from frost during the winter that followed.

Other crops were produced in much the same manner. For example, three or four acres were ploughed for oats. Horses did the ploughing and harrowing so there was not so much manual work at the beginning. One man sowed the seed, shaking it from a container, and sometimes artificial manure was applied. This crop grew, untouched by anyone, until August. When the oats were a beautiful golden colour it was time to harvest them.

Harvesting the oats and other crops was usually a communal activity, with neighbouring farmers helping one another. The corn or wheat was cut with a scythe or sickle, then tied into sheaves. Workers gathered the crop in their arms in convenient bundles, then took a handful from the bundle and wrapped it around the waist of the sheaf like a belt. You twisted the two ends together and tucked it under the belt from the top. Eight sheaves were propped against one another to form a stook. The crop was left like this for a period to dry. Later it was put into hand stacks and finally it was brought to the hay shed or made into a reek in the haggard.

In November, the threshing machine would arrive, something we children looked forward to. On our way home from school, we would hear its sound in the distance, a beautiful hum or drone like no other machine, and we knew exactly which house it was at. Each day this hum got closer and soon it was our turn. The men followed the threshing machine while it was in their townland, so eight or nine men worked together in a *meitheal* and knew from years of experience exactly what to do.

The threshing mill was set up in the garden, where holes were dug for the steel wheels so that the machine was stable. It was also very important for it to be level. The engine was attached to the mill by a long leather belt. When all this was complete it was time to crank the big wheel of the engine. White smoke and the smell of paraffin oil filled the garden. The engine kicked off with a ferocious bang, the workmen and children cheered, dogs barked and crows circled, squawking, high in the sky. They knew that there would be a feast for them later on. The man of the house pretended to be calm while he talked to the other men but inside he was bursting with pride. This was his day.

The most important job was to feed the sheaves of oats, grain first, into the mill. The sheaf was held for a split second, then released. It was a dangerous job and a good machine was always greedy to snap the sheaf from the operator's hand. I heard of a man who lost his arm doing this work: Pierce Prior from Augharan. A man called Miles McIntyre was part of the *meitheal* in this district. He was a tough cookie and fearless, or if he was in any way fearful he concealed it very well. Miles always took up the position pitching the straw as it came from the threshing mill. At one particular house, the threshing was almost complete. The man feeding the oats in gathered up the waste and fed everything into the mill, including an old coat that was concealed in the waste. Miles was at the other end waiting for the last straws and out came the coat in shreds. Someone asked Miles, 'Did you get a fright?' 'No,' said Myles, 'I was waiting for the man.'

Children and dogs followed the threshing machine as there was plenty of fun and laughter to be had. Donkeys drew the engine and threshing mill from house to house. These machines were hard to pull as they were heavy and mounted on steel wheels, so the asses got terrible abuse. Some houses had very bad laneways. In the late 1940s Harry Ferguson, a farmer from County Down, reinvented the tractor, which up to then was able only to pull, by introducing the hydraulic lift and pulley wheel. This was a massive step forward as the engine of the mill could be worked from the tractor with a belt from the pulley wheel. The tractor could also pull the equipment to the next house and the poor old asses were able to celebrate being made redundant.

Rats were a pest in the farmyard and there were plenty of them around when the last few sheaves of oats were disturbed. But men and dogs were ready for this. I remember being at one house for the threshing and a huge number of rats ran out in all directions from the end of one stack of oats. Dogs chased them, as well as people carrying branches. A quiet man who stood there taking no part in the action was Jimmy 'the Squealer' Gallogley. Then a rat ran up the leg of Jimmy's trousers and down the other leg to make his escape. This was at a time when underwear was a luxury and Jimmy was not wearing 'long johns' for the winter months. Another man, Michael Casey, saw what had happened and said to Jimmy, 'Good man, Jimmy, are you all right?' Jimmy let out a shout, 'Ah-Ah-Ah-Ah!' then collapsed in the garden. First aid was applied: a saucepan of cold water in the face.

The womenfolk were very busy on threshing day as it was a demanding task to provide meals for ten hungry men and a gang of children. There could also be babies or old folk to be looked after in the same household. In those days all the cooking was done on the open fire. But the neighbourly bond once again came to the fore when local women moved in to help: 'everything shared and nothing spared', as the old saying went.

Most of the yield from the oats went to the corn mill, to be ground into oatmeal for human consumption. This was another event I really enjoyed. It took three days to complete, as the oats first had to be dried on the kiln head. The kiln man was in control of this operation. He was a small man called Reilly with great pride in his strength and no bag was too heavy for him. He spread the oats out evenly on the kiln floor made of mesh wire so that no seeds could get through and the heat from the fire below eventually dried the oats. The kiln man kept turning the grain, a job that made him sweat. The farmer paid him either in money or by leaving him a portion of his cast of oatmeal so that at the end of the season the kiln man might end up with more oatmeal than some of the substantial farmers. When the oats were dry they were swept into another shoot and bagged and returned to the basement floor. The next day a hand-operated pulley wheel took them up to the third storey of the mill. Then they were gradually released down a chute and finally arrived in a hopper as the finished product, oatmeal.

I was fascinated watching the miller starting to release the water from the mill race and the big wheel turning slowly. It was hard to believe that this would transform oats into an edible meal. The big wheel turned a smaller one and so on so that, in no time, the smaller wheels where racing. The water mill was a wonderful invention with no running costs: just the water power flowing into compartments on the big wheel and turning the wheel at the miller's command. I count myself very fortunate to have experienced this process in my younger days.

Alas, these corn mills are now obsolete and derelict, although some have been preserved as a link with the past. A few years ago, I visited my favourite corn mill, Green's in Drumcannon, Carrigallen. I walked around this ghostly building where I played as a little boy and learned so much. I didn't venture into the mill in case some structure might collapse but I peeped cautiously and listened to the silence. From outside I could see the long bench in front of where the kiln fire used to be, where men, including my own father, sat and smoked their pipes and told stories while waiting for their rich harvest to be ground into oatmeal. At this moment, I could sense their spirits all around me, laughing and taking all the hard work in their stride. I saw the big mill wheel lying there, covered with moss and algae, its timber compartments decaying. I passed by a derelict shed, now roofless, where my brother Jack and I had played sixty-five years before. A startled bird flew out, screeching, as if I had been the only disturbance in a while.

As I turned away, the words of the song 'The Old House' came to my mind:

> *The children have scattered, the old folk are gone,*
> *Why stand I here, like a ghost or a shadow?*
> *'Tis time I was moving, 'tis time I passed on.*

When the oats were milled all the seeds were extracted and we took them home to feed to the pigs. The oatmeal was packed into larger bags, each holding about twenty stone, which were stacked in the corner of the kitchen, near the fire. The kitchen would now look smaller and the light from the paraffin lamp was somewhat eclipsed. There was a feeling of celebration as the family and the children finally witnessed the reward of the year's work and welcomed the winter months. We children awaited the first fall of snow and the frost, which opened up a whole new playground for us. In the winter there wasn't much outdoor work. Winter was a time to rest and reap our rewards.

Every year we put a few fields aside for meadow and loaded up the cart with farmyard manure, putting it in little piles around the field until it was dotted with heaps. We spread this out as evenly as possible until the field was fully dressed. No artificial manure was used for meadow at this time.

The best time for cutting hay was in June; in my youth the weather seemed to be far better than it is now and we expected to have several weeks of dry weather with constant sunshine. The hay was cut with horses and a mowing machine, although in the 1920s and 1930s it had been done with a scythe. Leitrim farmers have always held the crocket-handle scythe in high regard.

After the hay had been cut into swathes, it was left to dry for a couple of days, then it was turned with rake and fork to dry out some more. Once it was fully dry, it was built into proper cocks or wynds between six and seven feet tall. Súgáns or hay ropes (*súgán* in Irish) were twisted with a home-made wooden tool and tied down over the stacks to secure them from being blown away by wind.

The cocks stood in the field for a month or so and then it was time to bring the hay back to the haggard, the traditional storage area for crops. In most parts of Leitrim, farmers used horse-drawn carts but sometimes we saw a donkey and cart bringing home the hay. If the meadow was close to the haggard, the horse was hooked directly to the cock of hay to drag it home. This was a very exciting time for us children and we took up position on top of the cock of hay or on the cart if this was the conveyance used.

As with all the major jobs on the farm, a *meitheal* of up to ten neighbouring men worked together to bring in the hay. Then they moved on to the next house and everything was completed in the same manner. We children were welcome in every house and adored all the excitement. The tramping of the hay was a special treat for us, whether it was on a hay rick or in the hay shed. There were only a few hay sheds in our district so ricks were mostly used. The men on the ground pitched the hay up to the men on top and when the rick was made the sides were tidied up with a rake, with special attention given to the base. Finally, the rick was headed and tied with strong rope. Not one handful of this precious fodder went to loss. When it was completed, the hay rick stood in the haggard like a work of art, defying the elements, come rain or wind.

The old ways definitely took more time than modern methods but the exercise was good, the air was fresh and harvesting or haymaking were events that brought our farming community together. Nowadays neighbours pass one other in their motor cars, exchanging a fleeting wave of the hand, and so much is lost as we rush by with no time to stop and chat.

Harvesting turf for winter months was another chore that called for the participation of all the family. We started work in April. The first task was stripping the turf bank down to a depth of at least a foot and disposing what was stripped off into the bog hole left by last year's extraction of turf. The area we stripped was about five feet wide and its length depended on the supply we estimated we would need to fuel the home for the winter months. Cutting the turf involved two people. One cut the turf into small brick-like shapes and threw them to the other man, who placed the sods on a wheelbarrow and wheeled them out the cut-away bog. This work continued for a week or more until the required amount was cut.

Corroneary bog was renowned for its good quality black turf. It had also some poor quality, white turf, known as 'spadda' (from the Irish *spadach*) but this also served a useful purpose as it was easy to kindle to start the fire in the morning. Kippens (*cipíní* is the Irish word for sticks) also helped for kindling and *brosna* (Irish for dead or dried twigs or small branches) was a great help when the turf was of poor quality.

Working on the bog was a pleasant activity, with the workmen in close proximity so they told jokes and yarns all day. As young children, we really loved the bog: it was great fun to run around in bare feet, jumping bog holes and clamps of turf. As we got older and stronger, we wheeled the freshly cut turf out the bog. Lifting the turf and putting it into rows required many hands. Then the sods were put into clamps and when dry, were transported home in carts pulled by horses or asses and stacked in the garden or shed.

This work was crucial as turf was the only source of heat and fuel for cooking. The last chores of the night were to boil the big pot of potatoes for the pigs and rake the fire, covering the remaining coals with ashes and a few fresh sods on top so that it was easy to light in the morning. The skillet pot with the stirabout (porridge) was left hanging on the crook all night to be nice and warm for eating at breakfast time. Farmers also sold turf in the local towns, Carrigallen, Ballinamore and Mohill, a welcome income for the families who were fortunate enough to have good quality turf.

The women brought food to the bog, the only time this happened in the course of the year's farm work. The bog was a great place to work up an appetite and people who came from a long distance might start a fire and cook, sometimes frying bacon and eggs. The aroma drove the men on the bog crazy with hunger and if a supply of food did not turn up in good time, they would have to sit down with the hunger and weakness. Dinner on the bog generally consisted of potatoes, eggs, bacon and cabbage, washed down with mugs of milk. There was a five-naggin bottle of tea with paper twisted into the neck of the bottle as a cork and fresh soda bread to finish the meal. The womenfolk would gather up their accoutrements and go back home to continue the work of the house but the workmen would lie for half an hour or more grunting with contentment after this satisfying meal.

One man who took part in turf-cutting had a ferocious appetite and was always absolutely starving waiting for his wife to come with his dinner. There was no way to tell the time, as watches were an unknown commodity, but someone might hear the Angelus bell ringing at noon and the men would take off their caps to pray. Some of the men decided to play a trick on the hungry man: they took their caps off at around eleven and prayed. After an hour the man started to look out for his wife but there was no sign of her and, to his fury, she did not arrive until an hour later. She had a terrible job convincing him that it was only one o'clock. All he could think of to say was: 'It's a long time since those men said the Angelus.'

Owen Brennan from Augharan specialised in cutting a large amount of turf each year. He bought a turf bank from Mrs Downey of Corroneary, which didn't seem to be very big but had a depth of twenty feet or more of the best quality turf in Corroneary bog, with no water interference. It had cut-away rights for 'rearing' (drying or saving) the turf. Owen would arrive early in the morning with his son Pat and his ass cart loaded with supplies: bacon, eggs, vegetables, potatoes and bottles of new milk. They also brought hay and oats for the ass. This ass had a task like no other animal on the bog. It was hooked to a home-made contraption known as a 'slipe', which had wooden rollers on the bottom about nine inches in diameter that made it very easy to pull. There was a hinged door about 4'x4' on the floor of the slipe. When it was loaded with newly-cut turf the ass would pull the consignment to the cut-away bog for drying. All Owen had to do was to catch the turf as it was cut, stack it on the slipe, guide the ass to the cut-away bog and lift the door, using the two projecting handles. The turf would slide off gently, undamaged.

Owen's son Pat, who was then about fifteen, was one of the best turf cutters on Corroneary bog. He lowered the turf bank in three segments, taking the turf off the gravel in the last segment. Nothing went to loss with this father and son. They worked as if everything were prearranged. The fire was lit at noon and the two men took turns preparing the meal. They took an hour to eat and rest and they took great care of the ass. The Brennans always had a great supply of bacon and nothing was rationed for this visit to the bog. Pat Brennan emigrated to the USA in the 1950s and established a large building contracting firm in Connecticut, where he lives to this day.

As I write, Corroneary bog is deserted. Shrubs and birch trees devour a new part of it every year and it has been used for unofficial dumping of waste, although not by local people. But the gallant local community formed a committee and installed a locked gate on the pass leading to the centre of the bog. Keys are available to anyone who has access to the bog but outsiders are not welcome. The bog is now a home to wildlife and nobody cuts turf there in the traditional way. Once this bog was alive with happy voices: laughing, shouting, cheering and the sound of children playing. Now the only sounds that disturb the silence are the humming of bees, the sharp cry of the snipe or the yelp of a vixen.

The EU has banned turf-cutting on the bogs of Ireland but I can tell you that nobody stopped anyone from cutting turf on Corroneary, Cloone or Gortlettra bogs. There is no longer anyone to take up the spade and wheelbarrow to harvest this crop. It is either a big John Deere or nothing.

6

Butter and Bacon

When I was a child, people living in rural Ireland were better off than those living in towns. We were almost self-sufficient as regards food: we had our own potatoes, vegetables, milk, eggs and butter, as well as home-cured bacon. Butter was made in a churn. There were different types of churn but the most common was one shaped like a creamery can. It had a fitted wooden lid with a hole in the centre, which allowed the handle of the dash to be plunged up and down until the butter was made. Another wooden device, known at the 'juggler', again with a hole in the centre, was placed over the lid to stop the milk from splashing out.

Preparation for churning was very important. Firstly, milk was stored in a cool place for a few days, then the cream removed with a saucer-like implement and put into the clean churn. Everything had to be scalded before this work began. Churning took about three-quarters of an hour, with all the family members taking a turn or 'bash'. Any neighbours or strangers who entered the house while this work was going on would have to put their hand on the dash. There was a superstition that if someone did not do this, the churning would not give a good yield or the butter might not come at all. In earlier times it was believed that if someone left the house while this operation was taking place without blessing the work or leaving a hand on the dash, this person could go home and churn and would receive a double yield of butter. This pishogue or superstition was known as 'taking the neighbour's butter'.

When the butter finally arrived it was seen on the handle of the dash and the first words uttered were, 'Thanks be to God.' It was easy to remove the butter as it floated on top of the buttermilk. The butter was strained off through muslin cloth and placed on a large plate with some cold spring water sprinkled on it to make it firm. Some spring wells in the district were noted for their special capacity to firm the butter. Then it was made into blocks with little wooden spades, again scalded with boiling water. The finished product was decorated with a flower design imprinted by another wooden spade or stamper and supplied the house with lovely yellow butter for some time; any surplus was sold. I remember my mother selling some of our surplus butter to Bradshaw and Clarke of Mohill and Jack Smith of Carrigallen. The buttermilk that remained after the butter was churned was not wasted but used for baking bread. It was also used for drinking with meals or as a thirst-quencher for workers on the bog. The buttermilk that is sold in supermarkets today bears little resemblance in taste and texture to the farm buttermilk of my childhood years.

Most farms kept a sow that was fed on scraps, or if there was a good harvest of potatoes she would get a share of them. From the sow the farmer would get two litters of piglets per year, the size of the litter varying from six to as many as twelve. In my youth it was common practice to bring the sow into the kitchen when she was about to give birth, in order to protect the piglets. A family member stayed up all night watching the litter in case the mother pig lay on one of the piglets or snapped at one of them and ate it if it strayed up to her snout while she was still in labour.

If the sow had more than twelve piglets, the extras were reared as pets, fed with bottle and teat. These surplus pigs were given to the neighbours, a welcome gift. A family sometimes hung the pet pig in a bag from the crook in the hearth so it stayed dry and warm. The more piglets the sow produced the better the family could live. Pigs were killed and their meat cured for the house, something that required considerable knowledge and skill.

There was always someone in the district who was particularly skilled at killing the pig and preserving the meat in a manner that would produce excellent bacon. James Gallogley of Carrigavoher was one such man. It was another occasion on which neighbours helped one another as there might be two or three men present, and everyone knew which family was next to kill their pig. The killing of the pig was a public event and children enjoyed it.

The pig was fasted from the day before, getting only drinking water. The killing was a humane operation and was over in minutes. The pig was given some food and while he was eating he was hit with a timber mallet on the forehead and knocked unconscious. The jugular vein was severed and the blood collected to make puddings.

The dead animal was then tied to the rafters with a rope around his back leg. The intestines were removed by slitting the pig's belly open and the heart, liver, kidneys and feet (crubeens), collectively known as 'griskins', were set aside to be delivered to the neighbours later on. The lard was also removed, melted down and stored in jam pots, to be used for frying during the year. The carcase was placed on a well-washed and scoured table and the head and all the bones removed. The pig meat was cut into sections, well salted and placed on a cold cement floor. There it would stay for about three weeks until it was declared cured. When this bacon dried out, it was stored in a chest and a portion taken out when needed and hung in the kitchen, probably over the door. The lovely home-cured bacon we enjoyed as a result far surpassed the bacon of today in flavour, texture and food value.

As children we were sent with portions of the spare ribs or griskins to neighbouring houses. These parts of the pig could not be preserved and there was far too much for one family. Families avoided killing pigs at the same time as their neighbours, as they knew they would get a share of the neighbour's spare ribs. We children would preserve the pig's bladder, a cause of great excitement for us. We dried it out and put it into an old football cover, then pumped it with air. In the war years rubber was scarce so the pig's bladder was a welcome replacement, even though it lasted for only about half an hour. We consoled ourselves with the knowledge that the next neighbour to kill a pig would provide us with another substitute football bladder.

The whole transaction of killing the pig and curing the meat was completed in one day, with nothing escaping except the squeal. Now, under EU legislation, it is illegal for farmers to kill their own animals, even when they do not intend to sell the meat.

Owen Brennan of Augharan, a skilled butcher, had his own abbatoir, where he slaughtered pigs for the pork market in Belturbet. As this was the pre-refrigeration era, all the work was done from October onwards, so that the temperature was low and there were no flies. A few men set out with asses and carts in the early morning to deliver the consignment of pork. In winter months, the roads were treacherous and, although the ass was a great negotiator of severe conditions, some hills were so icy they were almost impossible to get over. The men dug deep and with a combination of inventiveness and the strength and skill of the ass, made it to their destination. They spread their overcoats on the ground so the ass could pull the load. The man at the back of the cart would take up the last coat and run to the front with it. In this way the ass got over the frosty hill and the men applied the same technique to the next ass and cart. There was no such thing as defeat in the hearts of these people.

Owen Brennan also bought live pigs in different markets. One day he was at a market in Longford and bought more pigs than his horse cart could hold. He had a brainwave: he walked two pigs behind the cart until their feet give up. Then he put two fresh pigs to walk and loaded the pigs with the sore feet on the cart. He repeated this procedure until he arrived home the twenty miles to Augharan with his livestock.

A modern-day County Leitrim meitheal.

7

Cloone and Its Characters

Cloone is a lovely little village in South Leitrim that has won many accolades for its 'tidy town' activities. It is also famous throughout the country for its great agricultural show, held every year on August bank holiday Monday.

The village suffered a severe blow in 1800 when a new road was built from Mohill to Carrigallen. A Church of Ireland minister named James Eager, who had some engineering skills, directed the construction work. Unfortunately for the business people of Cloone, the Reverend Eager had some difference of opinion with William West, at that time landlord of Cloone, and he used his authority to direct the new road away from the village, leaving it at a great disadvantage in terms of passing trade and business. This new road was known as 'the broad road' and was probably the first ever bypass of any town or village in Ireland.

Cloone was renowned for its popular calf fairs, which were held each year on 26 May and 13 June. I remember going to one of these fairs with my father when I was about ten and thinking Cloone was a very big place. In those days it was all asses and carts and horses and carts that transported the calves to the fair so there were carts lined up for hundreds of yards and the street was crowded with people. Sellers would have to pay custom (a few pennies for each animal) on entering the village. Nearly all calves were sold; it was a very bad animal that would not be bought by someone. Buyers came from all over to this popular venue.

The calf most in demand then was a red white-head bull calf about six weeks old. You could get anything between £4 and £5 for this choice animal. Other calves, especially heifers, could be bought for £2 or £3. This may seem a very small sum of money in comparison with today's state of plenty but £1 had enormous buying power at that time. You could buy sixteen bottles of Guinness for £1, at nine pence a bottle, something that would cost you €35 today.

At one time, Cloone had seven licensed premises: Cregan's, Doherty's, Brady's, McNamee's, Kiernan's, Garvey's and Pope's. It also had two drapery shops: O'Carroll's and McGarry's. Pope's were builders providers and sold groceries and hardware. There were some smaller grocery shops, a blacksmith's forge and a cobbler's workshop. The village also had a post office, O'Higgins's, and a Garda barracks with a sergeant and at least two Gardai. Today none of these remain but the spirit of the people is stronger than ever. They now boast a new church, a great community centre, a school and a small factory, as well devoting some of their time to keeping the village one of the tidiest in the county.

Every parish cherished its own characters, who showed wit and humour and gave fast answers, but none could compare with two characters from Cloone, James Garvey and Peter the Blacksmith, who had a witty answer for everyone regardless of their position or profession. James was in Mohill at a fair one day. He had a good few drinks and was finding it very hard to get a lift home, as there were so few cars travelling. So James started to walk in the direction of Cloone, a distance of five miles. Not far out the road from Mohill, the parish priest, Father Frawley, pulled up and offered James a lift. The priest was a big, soft-spoken, placid man. James did most of the talking, of course; the few drinks in him were a great asset to conversation. When he reached the turn for his home, he got out of the car, thanking Father Frawley, and give him a pound to say a prayer for him. The priest took James's money and said that he would pray for him. Then he said to James, 'And will you say a prayer for me, James?' Garvey replied, 'Give over, Frawley. Of course I will, if you give me my pound back. Are yeh listening to me, Frawley?' (These were some of James Garvey's catchphrases.)

There were many other stories told about James Garvey's witty tongue. Once, he went to the doctor in Mohill with a sore toe. The doctor examined James and said that he had a very nasty toe and that he would give him some tablets. James replied, 'I know you will, Doctor, but what about my toe?' The doctor explained that the tablets were for his toe but James interrupted him to say, 'Aren't yeh selling tablets, Doctor?' At the time this doctor was a shareholder in the local chemist's shop. All the doctor could do was laugh at James's remark.

James had an aunt who died and left a small bit of property. There was no will and nothing had been signed over to anyone. There were many relatives who claimed rights to the property but according to the law it would have to be disposed of and the proceeds divided among the next of kin. Frank Gannon was the solicitor in charge of distributing the assets. He was a great solicitor and, although he was expensive, he was held in high esteem professionally. After extensive research, he called in all the relatives, including James, and explained to them about all the work he had had to do. There was not a lot of money to be divided and James's portion was very small indeed. Mr Gannon explained to the benefactors that the high costs he had incurred in sorting out the case were the reason that the amount of money he had to distribute was so small. The other relatives accepted the solicitor's statement with long faces. Mr Gannon shook hands with each of them and the last to shake his hand was James, who said, 'Give over, Gannon. Are yeh listening to me? Was it my aunt or yours who died? Are yeh listening to me, Gannon?'

Peter the Blacksmith was another great character. He could adopt the countenance of the devil when telling a joke or yarn but behind this appearance he was really enjoying himself. In bygone days, the priest in the parish collected dues at Christmas and Easter, as well as 'oats money'. This originated in the era before the motor car when the priest had a horse for visiting his parishioners and they were obliged to give a portion of oats to feed the animal. Then the motor car came into being and horse transport become obsolete so instead the parishioners had to give the priest petrol money to run his car. But the name of these dues had not changed; they were still called oats money.

This particular year, Peter had half an acre of oats in the moor. He tended to them very well and they yielded a wonderful crop.

He harvested the crop, cutting it with the scythe and arranging it in sheaves and then in stooks, and was very proud of his work. But at the end of August there was a freak storm, followed by flash flooding. One morning Peter got up to discover that all his stooks were knocked and almost covered in water from the flood. He was devastated and cursed the elements but he tried his best not to look into the field again and continued with his blacksmith's work in Annaghaman. People calling to the forge would enquire of Peter, 'Did the flood do you any harm?' Peter never said a word about the oats but his countenance would change and he would vent his anger with heavy strokes on the anvil.

The following month, Father Clancy, the parish priest, called to Peter. Father Clancy was a big, strong man who expected cooperation from his parishioners at all times, especially where dues were concerned. He said to Peter, in a somewhat aggressive manner, 'You didn't pay me any oats money this year!'

'No,' says Peter. 'D'ya see what I main, me dacent man? The last sheaf of my oats is hanging in the eye of Lourga Bridge three miles from here and if it's of any good to you, you can fish it out, because I'm paying no oats money this year. D'ya see what I main, Clancy?'

No doubt the priest made an abrupt exit.

8

The Emergency

History tells us that the Second World War started on 1 September 1939. Ireland declared a State of Emergency on 2 September and the Emergency Powers Act was enacted the following day, giving special powers to the government for the duration of the war. Our country remained neutral during this war. Éamon de Valera stood firm on this.

The war didn't register with me as a frightening event as I was only six when it started and Poland was a long way from our shores. There were only a few radios in our district and houses with radios began to have many more visitors. Reception was very poor. These radios were powered by two batteries, one wet and one dry, and the wet battery had to be taken to town every now and then to have it charged up. The result was that we were getting very limited information as regards the war. My father went *céilíing* (visiting another house for a chat) most nights and when he came back my mother asked him, 'Any news about the war?' To which he replied, 'They are bombing away.'

Soon the effects of the war started to reach us. Tea, sugar, flour and other foods became very scarce, so the government introduced a system that tried to be fair to everyone. Each household was supplied with a ration book containing several pages of instructions in Irish and English followed by pages of numbered squares, either marked with the product name (such as flour or tea) or containing a letter to be used for different purchases. Space was provided for keeping details of what was bought, where and when. Commodities rationed during the war included oil, coal, rubber, tobacco, tea, sugar, flour, soap and clothing. These items were scarce as they needed to be imported. People had to nominate one shop, where they got a minimum supply of food for the duration of this emergency.

Unlike Britain, eggs and meat were not rationed in Ireland, as people had their own animals to provide these necessities. There were people who crossed the border with Northern Ireland and smuggled foodstuffs back with them. One pound of smuggled tea could be sold for the enormous sum of £1 so it was worth taking a chance. It was a dangerous transaction and customs men would do a body search of people they suspected of smuggling in this way.

People devised substitutes for hard-to-come-by commodities: for example some people smoked beet pulp and I once witnessed a man smoking black button seeds – a wild flower produced these seeds after blooming. Rubber was also scarce and when the tube in an old bicycle wheel collapsed and perished with little holes in it, a common remedy was to pump in buttermilk. This worked for a while but the smell was terrible. Tea was replaced by all sorts of substances, such as carrots that were grated and boiled, then dried.

It was much the same in cities and towns at this time. There is a good story told about a Dublin family during the Emergency. The husband worked hard all week and on a Friday night he would relax with a good few pints. His wife had to ensure that he had a dinner when he got home, as otherwise he would knock the place down. She might have only one herring (considered at the time to be a substantial dinner for any man) so she would shout at the ravenous children: 'Dip in the dip and leave the herring for yer da.' Bread or potatoes and dip (a sauce made of flour and onions) was an acceptable meal for children.

During the Emergency our imports of wheat were curtailed, resulting in the introduction of brown flour, which had a mixture of bran, pollard (a fine bran-and-flour mixture) and barley. Even this mixture become very scarce so many Irish people had to fall back on meals of porridge, oaten bread, boxty and potato bread or pancakes. Our government introduced compulsory tillage, which required every farmer to till one third of his land to grow crops such as wheat, barley and oats. This was a good policy but it took almost two years before it showed any results. De Valera kept insisting that three items would see us through this period, 'the cow, the plough and the sow'. There were very few complaints from the public, no matter the curtailment or severe conditions. People were glad that the war was kept from our shores and helped one another out with good humour, although some did compose witty rhymes like the following:

> *Bless de Valera and Seán MacEntee.*
> *They gave us the black flour and the half-ounce of tea.*
> *They rationed the cocoa and all,*
> *But they couldn't ration the porter at all.*
> *They brought starvation to our little nation,*
> *So cheer up, St Vincent de Paul.*

We had an Uncle Johnny, my father's brother, living in New York, who had emigrated in 1908. He had served in the US Navy during the First World War and his son John Junior enlisted in the navy in 1943, at the age of eighteen. Two years later, when the war was almost over, he was killed in action. When Uncle Johnny got in touch with us at home, he realised the hardship we were going through as regards food and clothing. He decided to send us a bag of white flour, something that was totally unobtainable in Ireland at this time. About three months later it arrived in Carrigallen and I went to collect it with the ass and cart.

We had to keep this news from the neighbours because there would not be enough flour in this bag to make a cake for each of them and if you gave flour to one neighbour and not to another, you would regret it. So I started out with plenty of straw in the cart and old duds of clothes to protect this valuable consignment from rain and peeping eyes. The name on the bag was 'California Flour' and it carried the slogan: 'California fears no man.' I returned home with this precious gift; even the old ass was happy. It was great to get white bread again, although keeping it quiet was a problem. My mother used some of it as an added ingredient when she made boxty. She shared it with the neighbours and they couldn't understand why her boxty was so different from theirs.

The bag of flour did not last long. Some of the flour was mixed with the pollard and bran, to help the bread rise. Not alone was it impossible to make bread of pollard and bran rise; even when it was baked, it had a black, sticky stripe running through the middle which was impossible to eat. You just ate around the black and threw the rest away.

Oaten bread became popular, baked on a griddle, which was circular, about eighteen inches in diameter and made out of iron, probably by a blacksmith. One side was flat, which allowed it to stand in front of the fire. Housewives became experts at making this substitute bread. A housewife in our district renowned for the quality of her oaten bread was Sarah Owens. Everyone wanted to sample her bread; even the teachers at school would ask her children to give them a portion of this valuable cake. Menfolk walking to the fairs with their cattle would always bring oaten bread with them to protect them from the '*féar gortach*' (hunger). If they did not sell their cattle and had no money to buy food, they would walk home again with only the oaten bread for sustenance.

England was more than willing to purchase any surplus food produced in Ireland. There was a great demand for dairy and poultry products – eggs butter, chickens, ducks and turkeys – so much so that you could sell even an old, sick hen. You could also sell rabbits, hares, pigeons and any other edible wildlife. Even blackberries were in great demand We children roamed the countryside in late summer picking this fruit that had previously had no value and the fowl buyer would pay us for it.

Clothes and shoes were impossible to replace during the war. There were not in the shops; it was as simple as that. Clogs were used as substitutes for shoes. A clog was a type of footwear made partly or completely from wood. It had a wooden sole and made a terrible noise when you walked. There was no left or right foot: just a piece of flat timber cut out in the shape of one's foot. You could get the soles in the sawmill and if you had boots at home with soles worn beyond repair, the upper section of the boot could be tacked on to the wooden clog sole. The menfolk were transformed into cobblers against their will. There was an iron last (a piece of cobbler's equipment for holding the shoe in place) in every house but often there was no oil for the lamp at night so these unqualified cobblers cut the fingers off themselves trying to turn clogs into wearable footwear. Swear words were amplified in every kitchen.

I remember being sent to the blacksmith with the handles of six galvanised buckets. The buckets had long since rusted but the handles were in perfect condition and in this lean era, nothing was thrown away. The objective was to have them made into the shape of the clog sole with holes punched in them so that they could be tacked securely on to the wood. A piece of old bicycle tyre was attached to the centre of the timber to 'hearten' it: this greatly reduced the noise of the clogs. A piece of a Nugget shoe polish tin was tacked on to the front of the clog to protect it from wear and tear. The thongs or leather strips that tied these shoe replacements were known as 'whangs'. They were much stronger than modern laces and, after being saturated in linseed oil, they would last for years.

Because new clothes were impossible to acquire, the females of the household became busy, sewing, darning, patching and knitting. It was a common sight to see men with the seat of their pants replaced, sometimes by a piece of material of a different colour, a big circle like a dart board without the numbers. The knees, elbows and other parts of clothes were patched, and shirt collars were turned inside out and displayed as new. Some of our neighbours, who were lucky enough to have family members in the USA, were able to look forward to receiving a parcel of old clothes. When such a parcel arrived, all the family gathered around in anticipation, with children grabbing at garments and saying, 'That's mine.' Some garments were ripped apart before they ever emerged from the parcel. American clothes were different from ours and garments were often far too big: you could fit two men into one American shirt. All our people were slim at this time: 'Operation Transformation' was at the end of the loy, the scythe and the spade.

9

Rural Electrification and the Big Snow

In 1946, an announcement was made that a rural electrification scheme was about to bring electricity to the area from Mohill to Carrigallen. All households, dwellings and business premises along the way would have the opportunity to link into the service, free of charge. Up to then, light was a miserable candle or paraffin oil lamp; the best light was from the tilly lamp, if you were fortunate enough to get your hands on one, but normally only shops, churches, dance halls and other commercial premises were able to acquire such advanced equipment. I knew of a priest's housekeeper who collected the wax from the offertory candle display and melted it down. She poured the liquid into an old bicycle pump chamber with a string going through the middle, producing another usable candle.

In 1947, the miracle began that would change the life of country people for ever. But even miracles have teething problems. A majority of the people did not want to change. Most country houses were then thatched and fear of fire gripped the community in a big way. There was also another obstacle: 'ground rent'. In the past rents and rates were associated with landlords and British rule. Failure to meet these impositions meant only one thing: eviction. As a result, many country people had developed a phobia about rents and rates.

Meeting after meeting was held all over the country. I remember being at one in Maguire's hall, Corroneary, in 1946, when I was thirteen. There was uproar, with people objecting and condemning the proposed electrification. At the end of this meeting a foresightful man, Leo McLendon from Cloone, spoke. He advised all farmers to avail of this free installation of electricity as it would never come free again. How right he was. Most people at the meeting listened attentively and agreed with what he said, although some still declined the offer. Rural electrification was a step forward and our country was much the better for it.

ESB personnel became busy measuring the length and breadth of every house. This would determine the ground rent. One day when Peter the Blacksmith came home for his dinner, the ESB engineers were measuring his house. He enquired of them, 'What are you doing there?'

'We're measuring your house,' the ESB man said. 'Aren't you getting in the light?'

'No,' says Peter, 'I'm not getting in the light.'

'And why are you not getting in the light?'

Peter replied, 'D'ya see what I main, me dacent man. I'm married to a very big woman and we do have the occasional row and the less light she has the longer Peter will live. D'ya see what I main?'

Work continued on this project during 1947 and 1948 and many men from the parishes of Cloone and Aughavas got work on the scheme. This included digging the holes for the poles carrying the lines. They had to be put down six feet and a man digging had to be able to sink one hole per day with spade and shovel, regardless of the subsoil he met. The hole was dug in a 'V' shape about six feet long and four feet wide, allowing the man digging space to get down and manoeuvre his equipment. The last foot or so was in the narrow end of the V and was equal to the circumference of the pole. There were no mechanical diggers at this time.

The poles had to be brought through the fields by a horse pulling them along the ground. I remember the horse well; he was a Clydesdale that had been trained to pull timber out of the forest and if the pole became inhibited in any way he would change the direction in which he was pulling. Hubie Doherty from Cloone was in charge of this animal and he would stable him at whichever house was close to his work. The ESB paid two shillings per night for the upkeep of the horse so plenty of people offered to keep him and avail of this generous contribution.

Poles were erected by manpower with ropes guiding the manoeuvre and a group of men always making sure that the pole was erected plumb and in line with the other poles. Only then would the back-filling begin, again men using forks and shovels. Some of the men would eat in our house. They would ask to have the kettle boiled, then they would come in and eat their sandwiches. As a young lad I got to know them very well: Pee Donoghue, Esker, Cloone; Jimmy Joe McLoughlin, Annaghbrennan, Cloone; and J.P. Newton of Drumod. They were powerful workmen and it would do you good to see them sink a hole with loy and shovel in the specified time.

I remember watching a man assembling the cross ties on the poles that carried the wires. It was January 1947 and a cold easterly wind was blowing. He was Peter Higgins, from Corriga. These cross ties were put on with bit and brace before the pole was erected. I thought that he had a lovely job in comparison with the other workmen who were covered in muck from head to toe and always under the ganger's watchful eye. Peter was a lovely man and I spent several hours with him every day, sometimes carrying some of his tools as he went from one pole to the next.

It took more than a year to complete the project and the night of the big switch-on there were plenty of problems. Some houses had been wired by cowboy electricians; they had only one flash of light and then a bang. This put the fear of God into householders and even when the house was wired properly, some would turn on the electric light only so that they could light the paraffin oil lamp, then they switched off the bulb again. It took years before the electric kettle and radio were introduced. This was an extraordinary leap into the future. One man in our district who educated himself as an electrician was Michael Casey. Any house that was wired by Michael was done to perfection and he was called on for many years to repair botched work done by other electricians. Even the ESB recognised his great work.

The greatest snowfall of the century began on the night of Monday 24 February 1947. The memories flood back as I think of the time I was a lad of fourteen. For weeks before, an arctic easterly wind had been blowing across the land and snow was the topic on everyone's lips. As I went to bed that night, the first flakes were beginning to fall. It continued to snow for twenty-four hours nonstop. When I looked out the next morning I could barely recognise the farmyard or the countryside. Hedges and bushes looked completely different and some had disappeared entirely. It was still snowing heavily.

The snow of 1947 is on record as the greatest snowstorm ever witnessed in Ireland. I remember it as if it were just last year and I have never seen anything like it in the past sixty-five years. At first the snow started to fall like salt, very fine. The blizzard was driven by a fierce easterly wind that swept the countryside. It paralysed road and rail services and brought all traffic to a standstill. Similar conditions were being reported all over the country, with huge snowdrifts, some up to fifteen feet high. Everyone thought this was the end of the cold spell and that snow at this time of year wouldn't last long and that spring was just around the corner. But what a shock we got.

It was impossible to get to some dwellings but, as ever, the bond between neighbours manifested itself. People struggled to visit the next-door neighbour and so on, until everyone was accounted for. It was a task even to get to the animals in the outhouses and water became scarce because of the frozen ground. We took buckets of snow into the kitchen and melted it on the fire. You would be surprised at the small quantity of water produced by one bucket of snow and then, how could such nice, white, clean-looking snow produce such dirty black water? As the weather worsened, people began to face hardship, especially farmers who were running out of fodder. Because of the general scarcity of fodder, anyone who had hay for sale was getting whatever price they asked. Even the crop left over from 1945 sold well and hay reached the highest price in living memory, £1 per cut.

It was a great time to be young. We really enjoyed ourselves, getting up early every morning, hoping the snow had not disappeared. There was no danger of that. It froze hard every night, so we could walk and run on top of the snowdrifts. We made a sleigh from an old kitchen chair with a broken back and, taking turns, we slid down a long hill on it. It was great entertainment but bringing the sleigh back up the hill again demanded both strength and energy.

The exercise warmed us, although our noses were red and our hands blue with the frost. When we eventually went into the house, the pain started in our fingers.

Our laneway had snowdrifts eight feet deep on every bit of it but it made no difference as we could walk safely on the top of the drifts. With each passing day, the footpath got harder. I remember being sent to McCabe's shop for a bag of Indian meal. I got the old ass out and rode him on top of the drifts. On my way home with the bag of meal on the ass's back, things were different. Suddenly the ass disappeared and I was left with the bag of meal on top of the snow. Apparently the bag of meal of a hundredweight (eight stone) was heavier than I was at that time. I had a problem trying to take some of the snow away from the ass's nose so that he could breathe. We spent the rest of the day digging that ass out of the snowdrift, which was almost fifty yards long. We had no problem with the bag of meal: we just tied a rope around it and it slid along the top of the snow.

Regardless of the hardship, every incident that occurred was treated in a light-hearted way. Nobody complained, as living in this tough era created strong human beings with a wonderful fighting spirit. It created initiative to overcome problems and encourage inventiveness. These formative years stood to me and gave me the strength of character needed to deal with the tough circumstances life threw at me later on. I hear people say that 2010-11 was the worst winter on record and I try to tell them about 1947 but they won't listen. They tell me about their burst pipes, lack of electricity, that the car wouldn't start and that it was impossible to get it up the hill. I smiled to myself, thinking that, in 1947, there were no burst pipes or electricity cuts, no car, no toilets, no running water. The lucky few may have had a car but they could not find their car as it was completely covered for at least a few weeks and even when they found it, it was impossible to go anywhere.

During the snow the roads were all blocked and no supplies came to the shops. Leitrim County Council had workmen out clearing the roads and there were also many voluntary workmen and even children helping, enjoying the novelty. There were no newspapers in the shops and we missed our weekly *Leitrim Observer*. Radios were in short supply. The batteries ran down and there was no way of taking them to town to have them charged up again. So a new form of community news was established: people started writing in the snow all along the roadways. You could write or read anything there and it was all anonymous. At that time, courting couples would try to keep their friendship secret but if someone got to hear about it, they released the news for everyone to read along the road. I knew of two women in our district who used to walk for miles every day just to read about who was going out with whom or any other bit of juicy scandal. The person who didn't want their courting to be exposed in this manner had to be out early in the morning and drag a stick along the writing to get rid of it. The writing was there for weeks and become easier and easier to read as it was enlarged by each night's frost. I smile when I think of today's cyber world. Sixty-five years ago we had our own Facebook in the snow.

A man in his early eighties got married in January, just before the snowstorm of 1947. His bride was a woman in her early fifties and they had known each other for years. I served Mass on the morning of their wedding. It was very cold with easterly gales blowing. The groom was a decent man and he gave me a half-crown (two shillings and sixpence) for my trouble. I can still remember the emblem on that coin: a stylish horse on one side, with a harp on the other. Of course their marriage got full publicity on the snow Facebook that ran along the roads. One piece of writing was directed at the bride, wishing her well in the future years and hoping that she would not find 'old age creeping up on her'. When the snow finally disappeared in mid-April, all this communication was deleted, the writing became a distant memory and no one took offence for too long.

The self-sufficiency of the rural people came into its own at the time of the great snow. There was an abundance of good healthy food: potatoes, eggs, vegetables, oatmeal, milk and home-cured bacon. When the potatoes in our barn came to an end, we had to go to the field and open the heap of stored potatoes. Firstly, it was hard to find the heap; then it had to be attacked with sledgehammer and crowbar to get it open. These potatoes had been stored in the heap since the previous October. They were covered with straw or bedding, then with about nine inches of clay in the shape of a pyramid. The people knew that their very survival depended on the preservation of this vital crop as there was no St Vincent de Paul to call upon. It was a weight on my father's shoulders, with several little mouths depending on him.

After some time, we found the heap. It took another hour to make an entrance. Still my father worried that potatoes would have been destroyed by frost. Finally, he reached the bedding and to his delight, not one potato had been frostbitten. We brought home a supply of lovely Kerr Pinks to last us for a while. We secured more bedding at the front of the heap and rolled back the big squares of earth for further protection. As the frost continued day and night, we had to go again and again to the heap of potatoes. By the time the thaw arrived, we had gone more than four feet into the heap. This was a task the young were good at: creeping on their belly under the frozen pyramid. There was no danger of the pyramid collapsing until the thaw came in the month of April.

A lorry load of cattle coming from the noted Monaghan fair got stuck in the ditch just past Brady's public house. There were nine choice bullocks aboard. The cattle were all thrown clear but were then at the mercy of the snowstorm. The driver could do nothing. He didn't own them and he could not get in touch with the man who had hired him to deliver them. But all was not lost: the local people surrounded the cattle and soon everyone volunteered to take one bullock, as they could not release them to the violent storm. The lorry was in the hedgerow for weeks until finally the Brewsters garage men from Carrigallen were sent for. They worked for days trying to jack up the lorry. It was an old-time jack and every time it reached maximum extension, the end of it went down in the soft snow under the frost. The men put more stones under the jack and started all over again. Finally the Brewsters succeeded and with plenty of manpower they returned the lorry to the road. The cattle stayed with their adopted owners until the road was usable again, then the owner came and collected them, more than grateful to the people who took care of them. There was no word of compensation and none was expected, such was the bond that these rural people had with cattle and other animals.

Later on in my life, in the 1960s, the buzzword with builders and developers was 'insulation'. I often laugh to myself when I think about the great people who went before us. They didn't know the meaning of the word and they definitely would not have been able to spell it. But they knew how to protect their potatoes and crops from the frost and the other elements. Take a bow, you wonderful people.

Andy in his home territory in County Leitrim. (Photo: James Connolly, the Irish Independent*)*

10

The LDF/FCA

The LDF was a local force to defend our country against being invading by the Germans. Young men and boys joined the force and trained in the local halls at night. Their main weapons were the rifle, the bayonet and the grenade: they used wooden guns for drill practice and the .303 rifle for shooting practice. I remember seeing a wooden replica rifle during the war, when I was nine.

Regular army personnel came to our area to train the LDF in manoeuvres, such as running through the fields camouflaged as trees and bushes that blended into the surrounding landscape. They carried out a training session in the month of November on the top of a jungle-like hill between Aughavas and Cloone. The troops participating in these manoeuvres were well spread out, with faces blacked. They ran to the hedgerows and took up positions with rifles cocked through the hedgerows, as if awaiting Germans. A sergeant from the regular army ensured that the manoeuvres were carried out satisfactorily and LDF members had to give their rank when the sergeant asked them, 'What are you?' The answer was a one-star, two-star or three-star private.

Most of the young recruits in the LDF were a hundred per cent committed to the defence of their country but they were also glad of the bit of free clothing: new boots, leggings, trousers and tunic. Best of all was the overcoat, a lifesaver on the bed at night equal to any blanket.

Jimmy Joe was a man who did his bit in these manoeuvres. He was very intelligent and knew there was no danger whatsoever of any Germans coming to this isolated spot, but he took part in running up the hill, well camouflaged, with leaves and twigs in his cap. He ran to the hedgerow and got down on the ground with his rifle sticking out through the bushes, awaiting the arrival of these phantom Germans. As he lay there, he felt dampness seeping up through his great coat. This was the coat that would be on his bed that night so he was enraged by this unnecessary training and moved a few times to try to protect his coat from the dampness. The sergeant from the regular army hit him on the heels and said, 'What are you?' Jimmy Joe, with a frightening look on his face, replied, 'A bollocks.' The sergeant could do nothing but laugh, as he too realised that this was the last place any German would appear.

James Dolan was another young man who joined the LDF and rose to the rank of corporal in no time. It was not unusual for a soldier to take home with him his rifle and maybe some bullets or grenades. One day James's mother found a hard lump in James's greatcoat pocket and he explained to her that it was an army grenade, a mini-bomb capable of blowing up part of a structure. His mother was nervous but James reassured her that he would first have to remove the pin, then throw the bomb by hand, making sure to be a good distance away from the target.

The mother became very interested in this destructive gadget. She said to her son that there was an old toilet at the end of the garden and wondered if this contraption would be able to destroy it as she hated looking at it. 'No bother,' said James, taking the grenade from his greatcoat pocket. He removed the pin and threw the grenade in the direction of the toilet. It reached the door and there was a terrible explosion. The entire toilet went skywards and when everything had settled, out of the cloud of dust walked the grandfather, his clothes in shreds, a replica of Jack Frost. He let out a ferocious shout: 'Jaysus Christ, it must have been something I ate!'

In October 1945, the name of the LDF was changed to the Irish version: FCA (*Fórsa Cosanta Áitiúil*). The FCA became active in our area and soon every parish had its own group. I joined up in 1950 and enjoyed every moment I spent with this organisation. We all got our clothes – tunic, cap and badge, trousers, leggings, boots and greatcoat. Some smart people called the FCA the Free Clothing Association; others called it Fools Carrying Arms. Everyone who joined started as a one-star private but with training you could rise to two-star or three-star, or even become a corporal in a few years.

There were two weeks of training every year at one of the army barracks. I remember training in Mullingar, Renmore Barracks in Galway, Finner Camp, County Donegal, and Athlone. We looked forward to this because we were well paid and money was scarce at home. We always arranged this training session for November, in order to have money for Christmas. The weekly pay was only about £3 but there was also a weekly gratuity, so that the total came to £20 or more. It was an enormous amount of money for us to have approaching Christmas and as we were paid on the last day of our training we didn't have the opportunity to spend it.

The training supplied by the FCA was also of great value to us. It taught us how to walk, march and keep our uniform clean and respectable. We also had to make our own beds and protect the most important utensils that were given to us: knife, fork and spoon. We learned how to use firearms and to respect them. We went to Finner Camp for a shooting competition and range practising, something I really enjoyed. We were given a rifle and five rounds of bullets in a magazine; we had already been instructed how to load it. We positioned ourselves, lying on the ground three hundred yards from the target and resting our rifles on some sandbags. Some of our colleagues would take up positions in the concrete bunkers (butts), from where the target would appear in the shape of a yellow man from the waist up, known in the army as the 'bobbing man'. The target appeared for no more than five seconds and if you hit it, the man in the butts displayed it again, this time spinning it around for seconds. This was repeated four times and if you hit the target five times out of five, you were declared a marksman and got a badge that would identify you as such. My neighbour, Pat Downey, was one of the few who succeeded in this test.

During this time young people lacked opportunities to mix with their peers in other parishes. There were no secondary schools, so the only way to meet people from other parishes was on the football field and that could be slaughter. The FCA lads from my parish trained with lads from all the surrounding parishes: Mohill, Annaduff, Bornacoola, Cloone, Drumreilly, Drumeala and Ballinamore. The FCA personnel from these parishes were known as the 'Mohill battalion'.

Today I often think of the benefits of that recruitment in our teenage years. I wonder if there is any way the young people of today could benefit from this training and discipline. It would be much better than the dole. It would make men out of boys, teach them to respect others and definitely get them out of the drug culture. I would even go as far as to say that there should be compulsory military training, as there was in England in the 1950s, when all the young men had to do two years of national service, something that freed them from their mothers' apron strings.

11

An American Wake

At this time, Maguire's dance hall in Corroneary, Aughavas, was a great social venue, where all the best-known bands performed. As with all dance halls at the time, the dressing room facilities were not the best but Mrs Maguire told the girls they could avail of the facilities in her dwelling house thirty yards away. The girls had to pass through the kitchen on their way to the parlour to powder their noses. Sometimes there was a sow giving suck to ten or twelve piglets on the kitchen floor, a sight to behold, or on their way back they might have to step over piglets running around. It was nothing they hadn't seen before and none of the girls passed any remarks. By the way, these were the best looking girls you could ever hope to see.

Boys and girls came from the neighbouring parishes to Maguire's in great numbers, using bicycles as a mode of transport as there were very few cars at this time. Admission was three shillings and sometimes even this sum was hard to find. The boys lined up on one side of the hall and the girls on the other. The bandmaster announced, 'Take your partners for the next dance,' but the band played for some time before any of the men made a move. It took some courage to walk across the floor and choose a girl out of the thirty or more waiting to dance. If your chosen girl said no you felt humiliated and embarrassed. But, as Tommy Moran wrote in the *Leitrim Guardian* some time ago, 'We all followed Jim Foy.' Jim was a super dancer and a great man for the ladies and none of the girls ever refused him.

The bandmaster sometimes called an 'excuse me' dance and everyone abided by it. A couple could be going out together for some time and an unknown person could tap the man on the shoulder and say, 'Excuse me.' I wonder how it would work today.

*The ruins of Maguire's dance hall, Corroneary, Aughavas,
one of the original 'ballrooms of romance'.*

As I grew into my teens, I was very sad to hear of some young man or woman departing for the USA or England. These were people I admired working at the hay, the turf, or the potatoes, or feeding the pigs or poultry. Everyone could not make a living from the farm and the haemorrhage of boys and girls from Aughavas and Cloone and surrounding parishes was constant. My first American wake was for Rose Owens, a neighbouring girl I had known since my infancy, who was about to leave for the US. She was a good-looking girl, with a nice figure and auburn hair down her back in a mass of ringlets. She was a few years older than me, like a big sister, only better. She never scolded me for any of my wrongdoings but encouraged me to be more of a brat than I already was.

I really enjoyed working with Rose at the hay, turf or planting the potatoes. I would go along with her to 'gugger', or put the seed into the holes made by the steeveen. Rose would stabilise each seed with the point of the steeveen and then we would move on to another row. It was a tedious and time-consuming task but humour and storytelling made it bearable.

Now and then Rose said, 'Sit there now until I get back.'

'Where are you going?' I asked.

'I'm going to "teem the potatoes" and don't yeh follow me now, yeh little monkey, yeh.' Soon she would return, smiling. 'Yeh know, Andy, nobody can ever stop wind or water.'

In that era nobody told children anything about the facts of life so we got our information from older children or from observing the animals on the farm. Of course we could not envisage our parents taking any part in this flamboyant exercise. When I was eleven or twelve I asked Rose for information about this taboo subject called 'sex'. She told me about her boyfriends and the antics they got up to. Laughing her head off, she said, 'Andy, you'll know it all soon enough. Just be patient.'

Then rumour had it that Rose was to go to America. I had a cold feeling in my stomach, for I had depended on this girl for so much knowledge that she was my stepping-stone into the adult world. Already she had helped me to develop self-confidence and I had no problem talking to other girls. I knew that the preparations for going to America took a lot of time, up to a year in some cases, so I decided I would work with Rose and talk to her as much as I could before she left.

I was coming up to fifteen when the time came for Rose to leave. My father said to me, 'You'll have to go to that dance in Owens's tonight and, anyway, it's time you started going to dances.' That was the only education I ever got from my parents as regards the facts of life. So I dressed for this great occasion, shaving off the few black hairs on my top lip in the hope that it might encourage a few more to sprout. With a spring in my step, I set off. The Owens's house was full. All the neighbours, young and old, were there. The American wake was a sad occasion, as some of these early emigrants never returned. There were eight children in Rose's family and she was the first to go.

A fiddler, Joe Cooney, rasped away at his instrument, trying to get it in tune with the accordion. Finally, the musicians began to play 'The Moon Behind the Hill'. The sound of feet tapping on the cement floor was much louder than the music but the crowd got into better humour and a few people started to dance. Later, blue-rimmed mugs of tea were passed around, followed by plates of loaf bread and raspberry jam and, finally, sweet cake.

I sat quietly in the corner, involved in nothing except my duty to the sweet cake. This was my first night out among adults and I was trying to take it all in. But a beautiful girl called Maureen Doherty, a relative of Rose from the village of Cloone, was at this gathering. She was in her early twenties, fashionably dressed and full of confidence and, no doubt, attracting the attention of every young male in the house. She moved through the crowd, talking to all the young men but not staying long with any of them, much to their disappointment. Then she came across the floor in my direction. 'She must be going to talk to the man sitting beside me or to Joe Cooney, the musician on my left,' I thought. What a shock I got when she bent down beside me and said, 'Well, Andy?'

The next thing I knew, she had her arms around my neck and was kissing me. Yes, me. This was no peck on the cheek, as her moist lips pressed hard against mine. The crowd cheered and laughed. I was absolutely mortified but did not resist. At least, while the kiss continued, I was sheltered from the peeping eyes. Nobody could see my face and it gave me time to regain my composure.

At last she released me, stood upright and, smiling, enquired, 'How did you like that, Andy?'

'It was all right,' I stammered. She moved on, laughing. I felt like giving her a kick to help her on her way but I knew that this would be the wrong thing to do, as it would only draw more attention to my already humiliated state. So I smiled at everyone, rubbing the lipstick from my mouth. Later, I discovered that Rose's father, Paddy, had prompted this girl, saying, 'There is no doubt but that's an old-fashioned buck over there. It's high time someone gave him a kiss.'

That June morning, dancing and singing continued until light appeared through the window. Much later, the sun appeared from behind a drumlin, its rays dancing on the kitchen window. A hand reached up to the globe of the paraffin-oil lamp to quench its light. There was a hush in the kitchen. Someone brought a wicker chair to the centre of the floor and Rose sat on it, smiling. Everyone in the room joined hands and formed a circle, singing, ' Now Is the Hour When We Must Say Goodbye'.

The room door creaked. Rose's mother, Sarah, was seen making her way to the bedroom, face in hands. The singing continued: 'Soon you'll be sailing far across the sea.' Again the room door creaked, Rose's father, Paddy, was next and the door was closed tight: 'While you're away, oh, then, remember me…'

Rose's head dropped. Her auburn ringlets were spread over her knees, the ends of her hair wet with tears and her shoulders shaking uncontrollably. In keeping with the tradition of the 'American wake', nobody went to comfort her as it was something the person leaving home had to go through. An urge built up within me to break through the circle and comfort Rose. This was the girl who had taught me everything about growing up, the girl who had planted our potatoes. Now, here I was, watching her suffer. But I refrained from breaking the circle. Had I not been made a fool of already that night? Maybe I was feeling sorry for myself; indeed, my loss was greater than hers. Came the last line of the song: 'When you return, you'll find me waiting here.'

People crowded around Rose. There were hugs, kisses, handshakes and claps on the back. I could hear people saying, 'We'll see you soon again,' or, 'I might be over there myself some day,' or, 'You'll come back a millionaire,' or, 'Good luck, Rose, it's well for you.' I kept to the outside of the crowd and, as people moved towards the door, I went with the flow. I could not bring myself to say goodbye to her and, anyway, I thought, she wouldn't miss me. After all, I was only a brat of a garsoon.

Slowly, I walked the quarter of a mile home. Corncrakes were singing in the river meadows and a cuckoo flew past, accompanied by a smaller bird. This was my first night out as an adult. I should have felt elated but I have never felt as low in all my life. I had got a kiss I didn't want, my first kiss, an unpleasant experience, and now the person I had depended on for so much was about to leave. But I would recover. As Rose once said to me, 'Andy, never count the times you fall but the times you get up.'

In the 1940s the journey to the US by ship took several weeks and a letter from there took as long again. Neighbours called to the house enquiring after Rose until the day her letter finally came to say the she had arrived safely and got work and was doing well. I never saw Rose again, nor did her parents, even though they lived for many years, as she never returned from America. So it was a real 'American wake' I attended. She married and had a family of her own and I believe she is still alive somewhere in the US, God bless her.

Sometimes I pass by the deserted house that was once a lovely, three-room, neatly-thatched cottage, a hive of activity, where eight children and their parents lived in the 1940s. But the children have scattered, the old folk are gone and ghost voices from the past echo to me from the ruins:

> Oh, Andy, stop and have a chat.
> You're grown-up, now. You're not a brat.
> Your memory is so clear of happenings in the past.
> Pick up your pen and record this fast.

12

My First Job

Leitrim County Council employed workmen every year on a temporary basis to attend to the roads, potholes, water drains and rivers. This work could last from a few weeks to a few months, if you were lucky. I got my first job with the council at the age of eighteen, labouring with a pick, shovel and wheelbarrow, or whichever implements were needed. The ganger was John Patrick Gallogey, a local man. An overseer monitored the work on a weekly basis and if the required amount of work was not carried out it would be added to the following week's specifications.

John Patrick Gallogey was the best boss I ever worked for. He was a gentleman who never abused or overworked a young man starting out. I well remember my first day working for him. He called me to one side and told me to light a fire, go to the well, get a kettle of water and boil it for the tea. He repeated the instructions for the dinner break. I was paid the same rate – £3/10 a week – as all the other workmen who were a lot older than me and more capable of heavy graft. John Patrick's motto was never to overload a young man with work at the start, that he would eventually see what was going on and repay you a hundredfold.

The part-time work sometimes ended in the spring, which suited me as I would be leaving it anyway to attend to the farm work, the potatoes, oats and turf-cutting. In the winter I got a job with the Leitrim Board of Works: working in a quarry, raising stones with crowbar and sledgehammer, feeding them into a stone breaker, then shovelling them into a ten-ton lorry for delivery for road repairs. The area overseer was a powerful man by the name of 'Red' Moran, a wonderful footballer and athlete. I remember seeing him at sports in Aughavas where he won a trophy in every contest he entered – the high jump, long jump, the 100-yard sprint and the 250- and 440-yards. He won the weight throwing, the bicycle race, the pillow fight – you name it. Nobody could compete with him. He was a great worker and demanded the same physical output from his gangers and those of us who worked under them. These gangers were tyrants, quite unlike John Patrick Gallogey. They would do their best to humiliate a young lad starting out, or an older man who was finding it hard to keep up with the forced work.

I heard a story told about a man who worked in the quarry, using his horse and cart to bring stones to fill potholes on another road. Some of the men who were helping to fill his cart deliberately put more stones in it than the horse could pull, then ordered the man to takes his horse out of the shafts. One of them got between the shafts, two more at the sides and two behind and in this way they moved the cart of stones up the hill and on to the road. Then they shouted to the man, 'Now you can put in your effing nag!' There is nothing more humiliating than to make little of a man's horse or his wife but these idiots thought this was great fun.

There was a good group of us who had grown up together and now worked each winter on schemes like this. We were approaching our twenties and could work as well as anyone. We were not afraid of any ganger and knew that while some workers were slipping back with advancing age, we were going forward every year. I remember working in Dolan's quarry, Beaghmore, where the ganger was Red Brady. He had the name of being a slave driver but he seemed to respect our group. He was older than us and a single man. We told him stories about our exploits at the dance halls with the girls: bluffing, of course, but he believed us. Our group consisted of: Noel Blessing, Mickey Blessing, Tom Prior, Jack Reynolds, Pat Charles, Jim McBrien, Pat Blessing, Francie McIntyre, Peter McIntyre, Peter Reynolds, Bernie McGauran, John Pat Donoghue and Sean Cooney, most of whom are now no more. May they rest in peace.

Some of our work involved making a hole in solid rock with a drill three-quarters of an inch in diameter with a diamond head. The drill was about three-and-a-half feet long and two men in tandem started hitting it with sledgehammers while the third man remained sitting down, turning the drill after each stroke. The diamond head was harder than the rock so it made the hole in the rock. Now and then the workers changed about so that each man got his turn to sit down. This went on for a couple of days until finally the hole was bored about three feet deep. A little water was added to keep the dust under control and it was time to prime the hole with explosives. An explosive cap was attached to the end of a long fuse lead reaching the bottom of the hole. The other end of the fuse reached a few feet outside the hole and the hole was primed with gelignite. The ganger, Red Brady, then lit the fuse. I can hear his command as clearly as sixty years ago: 'Run, ye fuckers.'

Every man ran for his bicycle as it took no more than a few seconds until the explosion erupted and stones were sent skywards to a height of forty feet or more. There was one man in the group who had a far better bicycle than the norm and he took particular care of it, leaving it up against a hedgerow and always in his view while he was working. On one occasion, a smart blackguard reached out with a short piece of wire, under cover of the hedgerow, and tied this man's bike to the hedgerow. When Red Brady lit the fuse we all ran for our bicycles but this man's bicycle refused to come with him. He shook the hedgerow viciously but there was no time to investigate: he had to run for his life and leave his treasured machine behind to face the peril of the imminent explosion. When we returned to our workplace the man's bicycle, most fortunately, was safe and sound and not a stone had touched it. He stared each of us in the face, looking for a clue as to who had committed this act. It was a good job he never found out because I'm sure he would have taken the head off someone with the shovel. And who could blame him?

The blast loosened tons of stones and they were then stacked in a heap, ready for collection. Later they were manhandled into the stone breaker and broken into two-inch fragments for pothole repairs. But first of all they had to be rolled down from where the blast erupted. As we rolled these big stones down, one of the biggest got up speed and was heading for Pat Blessing, who was working at the bottom. Red Brady let out a shout. Pat immediately reacted by opening his legs and the stone went right between them without touching him. Red Brady was not a man to praise anyone but this time he said, 'Good man, Pat, well done.' Pat looked up at him with a frightened expression and said, 'It was a split-second decision, Ned, it was the only alternative.' None of us was very well read in the English language but Pat's answer at a time of near disaster lived on with every man working in the quarry that day.

Jokes and tricks were an everyday occurrence and we were all victims at one time or another. If you were drinking tea out of a mug or cup someone would cast a small stone and break the cup so all you were left with was the handle, but with so many eating in a circle it was very hard to know who had thrown the missile. Soon everyone was drinking their tea out of pea tins or vessels made of other unbreakable materials. Your lunch box was also a target for intruders; you could find your lunch missing, replaced by a stone, especially if your mother was a good cook. So, like that man with his bicycle within sight, it was always better to keep an eye on your lunch box. It was all part of growing up.

13

The Magnet of Adventure

My late teenage years were spent helping out on the farm. During quiet periods I went to work with the council and I spent the weekends enjoying myself in Maguire's and Doherty's dance halls. There were plenty of girls. It was like shooting fish in a barrel: you couldn't miss. Now that I was in the prime of life I began to feel a sense of yearning and discontent. I thought there must be more to life than just survival. A sense of adventure was drawing me to wonder what was beyond my lovely Leitrim.

One Sunday night. I met a long-lost school companion, James McGovern, at the dance in Maguire's. James and I were the same age and in the same class and had got up to plenty of villainy. Master Lynch would shout at the two of us in Irish: '*Mac Samhrain agus Mac Samhrain! Seas amach*!' (stand out). We also became very skilled at the three-legged race.

It was great to meet up with James and we had plenty of laughs about our past. He had gone to work in a bar in Dublin after he finished primary school. We hadn't seen much of each other because, as he told me, he was working seven days a week, with only a couple of half-days off in the middle of the week, which were of very little use to him for entertainment. He said, 'I'm thinking about going to England. There's plenty of money to be made there. Will you come?'

I hesitated for a few minutes. This was April 1954. I thought hard. I was completely anchored to the farm work every spring, although I got very little reward for it, and I couldn't leave my father to do it on his own. My school friend was awaiting my answer. I said, 'I'll go with you but it will be September.' He thought a minute, then smiled and said, 'All right, I'll wait for you.'

I knew I would have a problem telling my parents as they thought the present arrangement would go on for years. I also had a girlfriend but I was prepared to sacrifice her for the sake of adventure. James and I decided to meet up at the all-Ireland football final at the end of September as nobody would pass any remark about my going to the match. I would stay a day or so with my brother Jack, who was living in Dublin. That way I could bring a change of clothes and there would be no protests or loneliness at my leaving.

Off I went to Dublin that Saturday afternoon with my little bag of duds. I was apprehensive and my heart beat faster. That night I went with my brother Jack to a dance in the Crystal Ballroom, in South Anne Street. I danced plenty, as it released the tension within me. When the dance was over, I couldn't find my brother so there was only one way to get back to his place, walking, as there was no bus at that time of night. I did take stock of the journey on the way in by bus and it didn't seem very long. I knew the direction, up O'Connell Street, on by Parnell Square, past the National Ballroom, keep right on the main road and this took me to Drumcondra. I started reading every road junction on my left until I found where my brother lived: Hollybank Road. There was no problem getting in as the door was always on the latch. My brother Jack arrived later and asked me, 'Where the hell did you go? How did you manage to get home?' I said I had no problem and that I had counted the traffic lights on the way into town. (I was fooling him of course.)

Next morning was the all-Ireland final between Meath and Kerry. I had no great interest in the game as my mind was on what I was going to experience in England. I also felt a bit guilty about leaving my parents in this manner. I met James and some of his friends at the match and we agreed we would be ready to go on Wednesday afternoon, 27 September.

We arrived in Dún Laoghaire to get the boat that was leaving at nine in the evening. James had a respectable case, I had my little bag with just one change of clothes. My brother Jack and James's friends accompanied us to the pier. I can still hear the sound of the siren as it signalled our departure into the unknown. As the Kerry playwright, John B. Keane, wrote, 'Many young men of twenty said goodbye.' It was goodbye to my parents, my family, the dance halls, the farm, the cattle, the ass and horse and the sow with her twelve little piglets, things I had been anchored to for so long. But right or wrong, the magnet of adventure overcame the sadness of leaving my home place.

We arrived at Holyhead at about one in the morning. There were crowds of boys and girls looking forlorn and apprehensive about the future, with big brown suitcases that looked as if they could hold more. I don't know if there were cattle in some other section of the boat but there were definitely cattle lowing at Holyhead and the smell of cow manure everywhere. I said to my friend, 'It's hard to get away from it.'

At Holyhead, we saw a long train releasing steam at a ferocious rate. We all rushed for it and it was hard to imagine that everyone would get a seat. But we all did. Some of the carriages had no corridor and no access to a toilet, just six people facing six. Soon we heard a few more hoots from the engine and black smoke filled the platform. London, here we come. We were crammed into our seats, people from different counties in Ireland but all with the same purpose – to better ourselves. The majority of these young people had never gone beyond primary school and had nothing but muscle to present as a CV. When I think of their unsmiling faces, it reminds me of the train journeys to the concentration camps of the Second World War. Today, as I write, emigration has started again but young people now are well educated and prepared to take up good positions. The Irish navvy is no more. But one thing education cannot take away is the sadness of departing from homeland and loved ones.

The train puffed its way slowly through the lonely, dark valleys of Wales, now and then stopping as if it was about to break down with its heavy cargo of human traffic. In Crewe there was a fifteen-minute toilet break, then we were on our way again. We arrived at Euston Station at about eight in the morning. This was a busy place, several trains releasing vapour with such force that it nearly took your breath away. Everywhere there was a smell of burning coal.

People were rushing in all directions and those who had travelled on our train were soon submerged by a sea of other nationalities, although on occasion you might spot a brown suitcase making its way for the exit, toilet or tea bar. It was great to get out into the open air, such as it was at a time when every household was burning coal. We went into a café and had some breakfast but found it lacked the flavour of the home-cured bacon hanging from the hob back in Leitrim.

We got a bus to Kilburn High Road. James looked around and saw a pub, The Red Lion, on the far side of the road and suggested that we go in and see what was happening. We each got a glass of orange juice and a fat man behind the counter, who was smoking a cigar, got into conversation with us. James told him that we had just arrived in London (as if he needed to be told) and that he had worked in a bar in Dublin. The fat man became interested. He told us that his company, Brady's, had several premises around London. He asked us if we were interested in working for him and of course we said yes.

Now, I had never been behind a bar in my life and indeed knew very little about the other side either. He went to the phone and when he came back he said that one of the company's pubs, the Queen Adelaide in Shepherd's Bush, was looking for two barmen. This man, whose name was Gillen, was the area manager. We finished our drink and headed for Shepherd's Bush. We were shown to a big room with four single beds in it, had a wash and tidied ourselves up to look a bit more respectable. At two in the afternoon we were working behind the bar.

14

The Luck Of the Irish

We were very lucky: we had a job and a roof over our heads, we were fed and had a good bed and none of this had cost us a penny. I wondered how I was going to manage this work. I had never seen a till before and all the drinks were different from those in Ireland, with a halfpenny in the price of most of the drinks. Luckily there were not many customers at this time of day. I studied the price of most of the drinks as fast as I could and James showed me how to pull beer. It was mostly half and half: mild and bitter. My brains went into overdrive as I did not want to let James down and, in fact, I was getting the same pay as he was: £5 per week, including our keep. Today that sum may look small but my wages, working under Red Brady for Leitrim County Council, were only £7/10 shillings for two weeks and I had to feed myself. So it was a great improvement on that and I did not have to swing a sledgehammer for it.

I felt grateful for the primary education I had received, regardless of the beatings. I could make up the price of a round of drinks in seconds because something we had learned at school were the three Rs: reading, writing and arithmetic. I often laugh at the young people of today, who have third-level education. If you asked them to make up a round of drinks in their head without a calculator, they would commit suicide and now the till tells them the amount of change to give.

There were two barmen working with us, also Irish, who had arrived not long before us. Peter Boyle and Brian Smith were from our neighbouring county, Longford. The four of us slept in one room and got on very well. We were fortunate to find that job as we didn't have to worry about getting somewhere to stay. So you might say that it was the luck of the Irish that shone down on us that day.

The landlord and proprietor of the Queen Adelaide was a man named Chris Murphy from County Kerry. He was a big, fine, athletic man. He always dressed well in a blue suit but did very little behind the bar. James weighed him up very fast. He found out that he was married to one of the daughters of the house and this was the reason he was the proprietor.

When he heard where we came from he started to laugh. He was a good footballer in his day and played for London. The London junior football team won the all-Ireland final in 1938, beating Leitrim. Our county had won the home all-Ireland but had to play London for the final. This was considered no more than a formality, as London had never beaten any home county in a final. I have heard it said that the Leitrim team celebrated prematurely in Barry's Hotel the night before the game and some of them drank themselves stupid. Chris Murphy told us that there were only three good footballers on the Leitrim team that day: John 'Nipper' Shanley, Mick Kilkenny and Red Moran. They were pioneers. He was right there but there was no need to rub our noses in it. But then he was from Kerry and Kerry people never change.

In the next few weeks I learned a lot about the bar. Talking to the customers was an education in itself. Our working hours were not very sociable. We were off from three until five every day and we browsed around Shepherd's Bush market. This midday break was no good to us for getting around. Each barman had one night off per week but it was always midweek and even though I went dancing, I was not meeting up with the weekend people.

We decided we would move from the job. James went out and got work with Firestone Tyres, near Chiswick, starting the next Monday. He said we would leave the bar, although I had no job. But James was the leader and I was very glad to tag along with whatever decision he made. We looked for digs near Chiswick and got full board at £3 per week. We left the Queen Adelaide on a Sunday afternoon with our little bit of luggage and moved into our new lodgings.

But we soon found out that it was not the best. Our room was about fourteen feet square, with five narrow beds. We shared the room with three other men and when we took off our clothes to go to bed we had to pull them in on the bed over us, as there was no place to hang them up. One enormous man was snoring, with a big brown cat sleeping on his chest. In order to use the toilet, we had to pass through the kitchen and out into the garden, where there was a makeshift outdoor toilet and washbasin. Not much of an improvement to the back of the ditch at home. After two days of this, I said to James that we should leave. 'Are you mad?' he said. 'We have paid our £3 and we won't get it back. (No wonder he did well in later life.)

On Monday morning. James went to work at his new job. I tried a few places but got nothing. When James arrived home that evening he was distraught. 'I'm not going back there any more,' he said. The fumes were terrible and he was inhaling black rubber smoke all day long. We decided that the following day we would go to Wembley, where there were plenty of factories. In North Wembley we got work at the GEC Electrical Company. James was in the boiler house and I was making timber frames for the fridges, appliances that were at this time in their infancy. We travelled the long journey back to Chiswick every evening, just to get value from our £3.

I discovered that our landlady had rented out the downstairs room and kitchen. She slept on the kitchen floor in front of the range and was always up to get our breakfast. In the corner of the kitchen was a heap of old clothes and one morning I thought I saw movement in them. I found out that the landlady's twenty-one-year-old daughter was sleeping under this pile of old duds. And we were writing home telling our parents and family how well we were doing in England!

On Friday morning, our last morning in these digs, the landlady was up bright and early with the usual breakfast for us: two slices of toast, a bit of rasher and a sausage. We pushed the rasher and sausage to one side and ate the toast with the cup of tea. She enquired of us whether there was anything wrong with the rasher and sausage but we said no. We were too shy and embarrassed to say that we were Catholics and did not eat meat on Fridays. What fools we were. But we were just living up to our teaching that fish marked every Friday of the calendar back in Ireland. We said goodbye to the landlady and thanked her. I felt sorry for her. It was her only way of surviving and her husband was probably long gone. But London in the 1950s was no place for sorrow or sympathy. It demanded the survival of the fittest.

Again we were on our way with our luggage. This time we ended up in Cricklewood Broadway. We turned into Chichele Road and saw a newsagents on the corner named May's. Outside was a big notice board advertising accommodation, work and items for sale. We started writing down addresses for suitable accommodation (room and kitchen) but we did not know the area or how far this accommodation was from our work. It was a cold November evening and everywhere was dark with fog and smog. If you held a handkerchief over your mouth and nose, in minutes it was black from the falling smog particles. We were both at a low ebb, not knowing where to go and worried about accommodation.

There was a loud laugh behind us and a hand on each of our shoulders. A voice said, 'So ye are here.' Standing in front of us was Pee Dillon from Cloone, laughing his head off. In our early years, there was always great rivalry on the football field between the parishes of Aughavas and Cloone. The players would burst one another and many fist fights broke out but when it was over they would meet in Maguire's or Doherty's hall and all was settled until the next encounter. Was it any wonder that the last person we wanted to meet in our deplorable predicament was someone from Cloone?

We told Pee we were looking for accommodation but were not sure where to go. He said, 'Throw away your paper and come with me. There is room and kitchen going where I'm staying and I'm sure the landlady will be glad to give it to ye.' The rivalry between Aughavas and Cloone died a sudden death on Cricklewood Broadway that miserable November afternoon in 1954. Off we went with Pee and he was true to his word. We secured a room and kitchen from his landlady for £3 per week, thirty shillings each. A glasshouse had been turned into a kitchen, with cooking facilities, cutlery and seating, but in the cold winter it was impossible to sit for long in this fridge. The bedroom had a gas fire. Pee and Mick Dillon were in the next room and Aloysius Blessing from Aughavas and Johnny Reilly from Longford had another room down the corridor. The McNally brothers from Drumlish lived upstairs, so it was home from home for James and me. Lady Luck had smiled on us once more. Willesden Green station on the Bakerloo line was around the corner and took us to Wembley for work in no time. Our wages were £10 to £12 a week, depending on overtime, and we settled in very comfortably.

The Galtymore dance hall in Cricklewood was only about a quarter of a mile away. It was a wonderful ballroom with great space. I remember only one ballroom in my dancing life that was bigger than the Galtymore: the Seapoint in Galway. During an FCA training session in Renmore Barracks in the early 1950s we had taken every opportunity to walk into Galway to dance in the Seapoint.

There were dances in the Galtymore nearly every night of the week and two sessions on Sunday. I remember going there one night. I was in great form with a new suit and as I walked down Walm Lane the adrenaline was pumping. I was young, fit and energetic, I had secured a good job and living quarters and wanted for nothing. But at that very moment a feeling of loneliness and separation came over me. Wouldn't it be lovely if I could return and enjoy these conditions at home? See my parents again, my friends and neighbours in Maguire's hall, meet up with Tommy Prior and arrange a fox shoot in the early morning in Corroneary bog pass? It was like a knife in the gut.

At that moment a light shone down on me and I looked up at a most beautiful moon that had emerged from behind a black cloud. I could see every image on its face and yes, it did represent the man in the moon. As in the song, I 'saw the whole of the moon'. I stared hard at it for a few seconds and the adrenaline started to pump again. This was the very same moon that was shining down on Corroneary, Aughavas, and the people from whom I was separated, including Tommy Prior with his dog and gun. I felt lonely no more. This moon would be with me wherever I went. I become anchored to it at that very moment. It was my connection to the homeland.

Christmas 1954 was my first away from home and I tried to push thoughts of the celebration as far from me as possible. Besides, how could anybody be lonely in the company of Pee Dillon? There were visitors from Aughavas and Cloone with the Dillons every night over Christmas: Joe Bohan of Gortlettra, Willie McGarty of Mohill, Noel Blessing of Aughavas, Jackie Murray of Gortlettra. In a few days, it was all over and I was glad to get back to work.

Football was a great way of meeting people from home. St Vincent's, a club promoted by the McQuade brothers from Drumlish, was based in Gladstone Park, not far from where we lived. Leitrim lads joined this club, including Aloysius Blessing, Mick Dillon, Noel Blessing, Pete Kilkenny, Ray Beirne, John Kilkenny and Mickey Blessing. They all won London championship medals with St Vincent's in 1954.

Willie McGarty enticed Leitrim footballers to join his club, Tara, and every Sunday we went by coach to the Gaelic grounds in New Eltham. Many great footballers, from Aughavas, Cloone, Mohill, Ballinamore, Gortlettra, Carrick-on-Shannon and other parishes of Leitrim proudly wore the green and gold Tara jersey. My friend, James McGovern, was a great organiser and brought many fine footballers to the club. Tara won the London senior championship in 1947, 1951, 1995 and 2003.

I was well settled into London life by the spring of 1955. I liked my work and even got promotion but the thought of spring back at home tugged at my heartstrings. For some time I wrestled with the decision of whether I should go home or not, until a letter from my sister, Rosaleen, made up my mind. I would go home in April and return to London in September. I told my friend James what I was going to do and he sent for his brother Tom to stay with him and help with the rent.

At the end of April I arrived home in Corroneary. What a great feeling it was to be home again. Nothing in the world is as good as a visit to the homeland. The first thing I did was buy a new bicycle in Bradshaw's of Mohill for £15. It was a beautiful machine, a Raleigh with a three-speed dynamo hub that would take me anywhere. There were still only a few cars in the district. Maguire's hall looked very small now in comparison with the great space of the Galtymore.

That summer of 1955 was magical for me. The harvesting of the hay, turf, oats and potatoes was no problem whatsoever. My father had cut down on output, milking just a few cows for the creamery. He went to the creamery every day, milk or no milk, as it gave him a never-ending supply of humanity to mix with. I had a wonderful time. I was out every night drinking, dancing, socialising and, of course, seeing girls. I had plenty of money to keep me going, at least for this holiday period. I enjoyed good health and felt the world was mine. One beautiful summer morning I arrived home at six in the morning and went quietly to bed. At about eight, my father called me to get up and give him a hand. The weather had changed and there was rain on the way. He had oats in stooks and they had to be collected before the rain came. I reluctantly obliged. I had a light breakfast and headed for the oat field.

We gathered the stooks with haste and put them into hand stacks in the field, securing them with some dry grass on top and roping them for protection against any gales that might come. I gave it my best, trying to conceal the effects of the previous night, but I'm sure the smell of alcohol clashed with the fresh morning breeze. As we secured the last hand stack, drops of rain started falling and my father said, 'That's a job well done, I'd have been caught badly only for you.' I nodded and smiled, not in any humour for a conversation at this time. He said, 'You had a good night last night. I heard you coming home this morning.' He was laughing as he continued, 'Enjoy it, son, but remember: once a man, twice a child.'

As we headed for the house and some refreshments, I turned that statement over and over in my head. What is he on about? 'Once a man, twice a child?' I'm a man and from now on, I will always be a man. I dismissed his statement as stupid. But many years later, when I was diagnosed with MND, this statement came back to haunt me. My father was right: I knew that I was on my way back to my second childhood. From the moment of our birth, we are under the care of our parents. We are completely disabled but the good thing about this disability is that we forget about it. From day two of our lives, we are emerging from this disability and by the time we reach our teens, we have almost shaken off the mantle of childhood inadequacy. We enter a period of strength and self-confidence and our attitude is that nothing can stop us now. But later on in life when we are subject to sickness, accidents or just old age, we again become dependent on the kindness of others.

Oh, yes, that summer of 1955 was the life. I met the neighbours: the Lyonses, Carrolls, Downeys, McIntyres, John Eddie Brady, Tommy Prior and many more. I had an excuse to visit the post office in the morning for the *Irish Independent*, to get talking to Bess Murphy and Nan Reynolds, the two lovely girls who worked there, and discuss all the happenings at the local dance halls and who was going out with whom. I had saved a few pounds in England and a pound went a long way in Ireland at that time, when going to a dance cost you three shillings and sixpence and you got a bottle of Guinness for ten pence.

But all good things come to an end. It was September and, like the swallows, I was preparing to go. This time there would be no stealing away but I felt heartbroken leaving my parents and my wonderful neighbours, girlfriends and boyfriends. I had to fight against these feelings, believing that I was a man of the world now and that men don't cry.

Young people from Leitrim were emigrating to England and the USA at a ferocious rate. There were a few lads from Aughavas who, after hearing my stories and exploits, thought they could never get to England fast enough. Their mothers begged them not to go until I was going back. I was now an example of prosperity but, if they only knew, I was on the linings. At the end of September I announced that I was going back to London. My parents wished me well, saying it wouldn't be long until I was back again. I smiled and agreed, fighting against the lump in throat and that cold feeling at the bottom of my stomach.

The new gang of emigrants joined me: Peter McIntyre, Peter McGovern, Michael Brennan and Francie McIntyre. I drew some comfort from their loneliness. I was the tough guy, I had been there before and I was prepared to lead. We took the train at Mohill for Drumod – this was the narrow-gauge line (only three feet between the rails) that ran from Belturbet, County Cavan, to Drumod. There we boarded the big Sligo to Westland Row steam train and, with the lonely hoot of the siren, we were on our way. A coal fire supplied the steam that drove the big pistons and the greasy smoke went streaking down the sky in an inky cloak. Cattle that were grazing close to the railway track would take off and run as fast as they could to get away from this frightening ghost rider.

In Dublin we had some refreshments and made our way to Dún Laoghaire, where we boarded the 8:45 evening boat for Holyhead. There was a queue to get on the boat and competition for seats. The boat was bobbing up and down like a cork in the ocean swell as we left Dún Laoghaire but I told my virgin sailors that this was normal. Again I was the tough guy. Waves hit the porthole window with force and Francie McIntyre was worried. He ran over to the porthole to look out and shouted, 'God bless us, lads, I can't see any land.' I encouraged him to come back and sit down, saying that if land was any good, we would not be here.

We arrived at Euston station at the scheduled time of eight in the morning, freshened up and had light refreshments in the buffet. I started searching for the various addresses that the others wanted to go to and set out with my cargo. Some went to Victoria, others to Brixton. Eventually I found these addresses and made sure that they were expected. They were good decent lads. I said goodbye to them and told them I would meet them some time in the Blarney dance hall in Tottenham Court Road. They thanked me profusely. I went on my way to Cricklewood Broadway with Peter McGovern, the younger brother of James.

James was a man who would help anyone out, providing they got a job, went to work, paid all their bills, led a good clean life and did not sponge on anyone. A phrase that he always used when out with a group was, 'Everyone gets their own.' Peter and his brother Tom got their own apartment and James and I moved into another room and kitchen.

We got work with McAlpine Construction in Harlow, well outside London. McAlpine's double-decker bus left Cricklewood Broadway at seven each morning and returned at seven each evening. When we had eaten dinner, there wasn't much time for socialising. We had to be ready for the following morning, so it was eat, sleep and work. I remember a young Donegal man, not long in London, who worked on this job and travelled the same route every morning. He slept on the bus into work and on his way home every day, never talking to anyone. One morning as we arrived at Harlow, he stretched himself, arms up in the air, and said, 'Man, oh dear, the night went quack.' This was his Donegal accent at its best.

Soon we moved on to another building job with Units Construction, a big housing estate that employed a lot of people. This job was again well outside London in a place called Abbey Wood. We travelled by train and it took us an hour to reach our destination. We were fairly contented with this employment.

James suggested that we return to Ireland for Christmas 1955. Although I had been back in London only since September, I was delighted with this suggestion. On a Friday afternoon near Christmas we set out for Euston, our luggage a bit more respectable than when we arrived in London. The station was crowded with Irish people on their way home for Christmas and the train for Holyhead was jammed to capacity but the atmosphere was a lot better than when we were coming to London. We set out on our journey at eight in the evening to connect with the 1.30am boat in Holyhead – or so we thought.

The train moved very slowly, white smoke billowing back the track. Nobody told us what the problem was but we supposed it to be fog. Finally we got to Crewe and the public address told us that we had a ten-minute break so everyone rushed for the toilets and the restaurant. When I entered the restaurant it was like a sea of faces but one face caught my attention and seemed to be looking straight through me.

I recognised the man as Phil Owens, a friend from home I hadn't seen in four years. Phil and I had worked together for years at the ploughing in Aughavas. This work required two horses, something no family had, so the only way to get the ploughing done for the oats and potatoes was to team up with a neighbour. Phil was a couple of years older than me. He was a great ploughman and taught me a lot.

Now here at Crewe station we met up again. We hugged each

other with laughter and smiles. He had come to Crewe from Nottingham to meet a brother-in-law who was coming from Ireland to spend Christmas with Phil, his wife and children. A voice came over the amplifier: 'All aboard the train for Holyhead.' We parted. I hadn't even had time to get any refreshments in the restaurant and five minutes later we were going in different directions. I never met Phil again. He died of cancer at the age of forty-three (RIP).

The Holyhead train continued its journey slowly in the darkness of the night, stopping and shunting in the lonely valleys of Wales. Finally we arrived at Holyhead at four in the morning, hours behind schedule. The boat was long in Dublin and we had to wait until it came back again to pick us up. At that time Holyhead was a dead town, with no shops, businesses, supermarkets or hotels, just somewhere people went through, either to London or to Dublin. What a boring time we spent in Holyhead until the boat arrived at four the following afternoon. All hell broke loose, as more train-loads of people had arrived from other cities like Manchester and Birmingham, as well as London. They had bookings for this boat and our booking was for the boat that was long gone. It was chaotic and one thing was sure: this boat would be unable to cater for half the people awaiting boarding.

James said to me, 'What are we going to do?' He wondered if we could get some tickets on the black market. I didn't know whether we could or not but I did know it was every man for himself. The stewards started to let people on board who had the right tickets and sailing papers for this boat. I had a brainwave. I joined this queue of people and pretended to be very drunk. When I reached the gangway the steward asked me for my ticket. I started to search, putting down my bag and staggering across it. Again he asked for my sailing pass. I muttered something in a slurred voice and the queue behind got irritable and shouted at us to get a move on. The steward was still looking at me, searching and talking to myself. Finally he said, 'Go on before you fall in.' So far so good. I proceeded very slowly up the gangway, which was about thirty feet long. At the end of it was another steward. Again the question and the search. The gangway behind me was now full of people and the first steward shouted to his colleague, 'Let him on. There are too many people on the gangway.' I was waved through and told to go down under, otherwise I would go overboard. I went ahead, still pretending to be drunk, and in the reception area I found a nice seat and sat down, securing my luggage. No need for any more pretence: I was safe.

Some time later my friend James arrived. He enquired how in the name of God I had got there. I told him I would never have made it if I had his pioneer pin. James was a pioneer all of his life and still wears that pin with great pride, although he made a very good living for himself as a pub owner by selling drink to others. He had purchased a sailing ticket on the black market. I don't know how much he parted with for it.

We reached Dublin at about one the next morning. We met up with Leo McGuirl, who had attended the same national school as us. He was waiting for Rose McCabe, then his girlfriend, later his wife. Leo had a car and took us all the way home to Aughavas. Peter McIntyre from Corroneary was also with us. The excitement of being home for Christmas soon dispelled the memory of the hardship we had endured on the journey from London. It was lonely for Irishmen who had to spend Christmas in London or New York or anywhere away from their home. Shane McGowan's 'Fairytale of New York', which is in the voice of a drunken Irishman, could just as well have been set in Birmingham, Manchester or Boston, where the Irish drank heavily to banish their loneliness.

15

Carrying the Hod

That Christmas of 1955, after overcoming many obstacles to be with my loved ones, I had a wonderful time dancing, drinking and visiting the neighbours. I wanted to meet so many people that eating seemed to be a waste of time. The weather was cold, with plenty of frost and snow, which made everything much better. James and I took an extra week off, presuming that there was no work on the buildings in England just after Christmas. But what a shock we got when we arrived back to our apartment at Mora Road, Cricklewood. Our cards had been sent to us; in other words, we had got the sack – the one time it happened to me in my working life. This was entirely our own fault as we had not let the agents know we were going home for Christmas.

We knew we would find work somewhere but first we had to return to the building site in Abbey Wood to pick up some wages that were due to us. When we arrived at the site office we found there was no chance of our employment being reinstated. We collected our wages and left to catch the train back to London. Then by chance we met the area manager of the construction company, a man called Johnny Fox. We told him the story about going back to Ireland for Christmas and staying an extra week and he said to go back to the office with him. In a few minutes we were employed again, this time working with the bricklayers.

We were given a V-shaped aluminium contraption with a handle about three feet long. It had two sides and a back and held about twelve bricks. You hoisted it on your shoulder and carried the load to wherever the bricklayers were working. These bricks were known as industrial bricks and were very heavy in comparison with other bricks, known as flettons. We were lucky there was no ladder work yet, as the bricklayers were just putting in foundations.

It wasn't easy, carrying the hod. It is supposed to be an unskilled job but in reality it requires a lot of skill and takes a few weeks' practice. You have to master such things as running the ladder two rungs at the time, not touching the handle of the hod, sliding down the ladder with your feet pressed against the outside and stacking the bricks without catching your fingers.

Neither of us had ever done this work before and after a couple of days James said to me, 'This is a hoor of a job. My feet are killing me.' But I thought we should persevere, as I believed we would get the same pay as the bricklayers. Then Lady Luck smiled on us once more. There was a severe frost and the bricklayers had to stop working. Johnny Fox brought us to another section of the field where he got us to put sand into the footings of houses. This was lovely work and on the cold frosty days we could warm ourselves working. The shovel in England is different from the one used in Ireland. It has a short handle, a wide blade and a specially designed grip on the end of the handle When we got used to the shovel the work was easy.

There were about six of us working in this gang. One was black and had just arrived from South Africa. He was about 6'6" and of very slim build. He must never have done any physical work, as, when he tried to use the shovel, he was not fit. He lit a fire and stood with his back to it all day. He would look up at the sun and say, 'I see sun but no heat.' One day a lad in our team threw a shovelful of sand on the fire, immediately extinguishing it. The black man thought someone had taken the fire away. He went berserk and if he had found out who had extinguished the fire he would have taken the head off him with the shovel.

I did various kinds of work on many construction sites during 1956 but I yearned to have another try at hod-carrying, especially with fletton bricks. There was no machinery that could compare with the speed of a good hod-carrier. The team was made up of nine bricklayers and four hod-carriers, two on bricks and two on mortar. The two carrying bricks were out in front, at least one or two houses ahead of the bricklayers. A bricklayer would be laying in the region of 500 bricks per day, so the two hod-carriers would be stacking 4500 per day, regardless of the height of the house.

That summer James said he was going to the US, as there was more money to be made there than in London. A few of our friends had already gone to New York, men like Mick Dillon, Aloysius Blessing and Joe Bohan. James wanted me to join him but I was reluctant to relinquish home, the neighbours and the farm work, the summer holidays and Maguire's dance hall. At this time you needed a sponsor in the US to prove to the authorities that you would not be a burden on the state. James had an uncle who provided him with this security and I also had an uncle in New York who sent me the sponsorship papers. But I declined the offer. It was the time of the Korean War and young men entering America could be conscripted into the army for two years' service. I was having none of that. Whatever about defending my own country, I had no intention of fighting a war for another country. I much preferred crossing the floor of Maguire's dance hall and taking my pick from among the lovelies who were there.

When James moved to the States I did miss him. In the two years since we set out on this adventure there was never a cross word between us. Each Friday the rent and the bills for groceries were all sorted out and every penny accounted for. James's brother Peter moved in with me and we also got on very well. Peter was five years younger than me and came to London when he was seventeen. He had already served an apprenticeship as a barman in Dublin and was very keen to make something of himself.

When he was an infant, Peter lost one of his fingers. Like the rest of us, he spent some time in the tea chest and one day another brother was experimenting with hammer and knife, chopping at the top of the tea chest. He accidentally cut off part of one of Peter's fingers. Another little brother ran out to the mother with the finger, saying, 'Peter finger.' Of course there was uproar but there was no such thing as laser connection to repair the damage. The hand was washed, disinfected and well wrapped up and that was it.

Peter was short a finger but it never came against him; in fact it was an advantage. He got a part-time job as a barman in the Queen

Victoria in Kilburn High Road. The head barman in the premises was Vincent Doyle, a young man from Roscommon. After Peter had spent a weekend working there, the manager approached Vincent and said to him, 'Watch that young fella.' Doyle asked, 'What's he doing wrong?' 'I don't know,' said the manager. 'I never saw a man hitting the till like him before. He's too fast for my liking.' Peter's short finger was responsible for the way he hit the till and no one could do it faster.

Some time after that, Peter got a full-time job in the famous Crown Bar in Cricklewood and was resident there so he moved out of our flat. In no time he was appointed head barman and later manager. This pub had the largest turnover of any pub in London; of course 99 per cent of the customers were Irish. One day a young man came into the bar looking for employment and Peter interviewed him. It was Vincent Doyle, head barman from the Victoria. Of course he got the job. The two men were delighted to be working together again and did so for many years.

With hindsight, I don't know how all these Irish immigrants got work in England. None of us ever collected dole as we had been told by our parents that we should earn our living by the sweat of your brow and not take hand-outs.

We never got any career guidance and we didn't know how to get a reference from the Gardai, the army, or the religious. We had only primary education and the experience of working on the farm, which was absolutely no good to us in cities like London, Birmingham and Manchester. We didn't even have a driver's licence that could be purchased for £1 in Ireland at that time, no questions asked.

Some of us tried to get work in a Vauxhall car-manufacturing factory in Luton, an industry that was in its infancy in the mid-1950s, but not many of us were successful as we had no skill in metal work. Francie McIntyre approached the Vauxhall employment office and the man who interviewed him asked him, 'What were you working at in Ireland? Francie replied, 'A blacksmith.' 'Then you would know the heat tempering of steel and iron? 'Of course I would,' was Francie's reply. He got the job although he had done nothing more than pass by James Heslin's blacksmith's forge in Corriga on occasion. But Francie knew that nobody would ask him to shoe a horse in Luton. Good man, Francie. Another man I knew approached Vauxhall Luton looking for a job and was asked the same question by the interviewer. His reply was, 'Tipping around with the ould fella.' He got no job.

I got a job working with two bricklayers doing maintenance work for London Transport. It was very easy as sometimes we would have to stop to allow carpenters, plumbers or other workmen to finish their end of things. It was just what I was looking for. It gave me time to get used to carrying the hod, a skill I wanted to master. I practised all the difficult movements. Soon I could run up the ladder two rungs at a time. I also learned how to slide down the ladder and load the twelve bricks, crossing each two for stacking purposes. As I stayed with the two bricklayers for three months, my shoulder was well tempered to carrying this load and I was ready to move to the housing schemes and get better payment. I said goodbye to my two lazy bricklayers and headed for Luton, forty miles from London. I went out the Dunstable Road until I came to a pub known as the Halfway House. I enquired there and was told that a housing development had just started down Lewsey Farm Road.

I approached the foreman bricklayer and asked him for a job. He asked me if I could carry the hod and I said that I would give it a try. 'Okay,' he said, 'you're on bricks. Go over there and you will find a young man carrying bricks. He will tell you what to do.' Now there is an unwritten law with hod-carriers: you don't pass the leading man but you must also keep up with him. I joined up with this new mate, a strap of a lad of about ten stone. He was English and although we talked a bit I got the feeling that he did not like the Irish. We got on with the work. He was leading. I kept behind him. Soon he got up speed; we were loading out a gable wall on the first lift of a dwelling house. I followed him every step of the way and he was still rushing, with no talk.

Now in my slack job in London, I had learned a few tricks, especially about filling the hod. It takes six visits to the hod, crossing each two bricks, to complete the loading process but if you pick up four bricks and cross them it takes only three visits. Now with this flash Harry demonstrating how good he was, I put my plan into action. I filled my load in seconds and stood the hod on the handle waiting for him to go in front. This happened a few times more, with me waiting for him every time. I was on his heels no matter how fast he went. Finally he said, 'What's the hurry?' I said, 'I'm in no hurry but it's up to you to set the pace.' He was now in talking mood and this finished the racing.

When I went for dinner, naturally I joined up with some Irish lads who had other work on the site, while my new mate went off in a different direction. One of them asked, 'How are you getting on with Dave?' and I said, 'I think I've got him subdued.' Then they told me that he was the boss bricklayer's nephew. I had no problem after the first two hours' work and he respected me from then on. A few months later, I moved on to much greener pastures. I knew that I had mastered this job and that I could hold my own with any experienced worker. I was young, strong, athletic and weighed about eleven stone. A heavily built man would be no good at this job: no matter how strong he was, running the ladder would eventually wear him down.

Another housing development was starting nearby and I secured a job there with no problem. Our team consisted of nine bricklayers and four hod-carriers. It was a long-term job and we got bonus money for our work. Again I was on bricks with another man and soon we were out ahead of the bricklayers, a house or two in front. It was a lovely clean job and with those summers of great weather, it was a free, healthy job. I wore no shirt or vest at work but my shoulder was well tempered and did not even mark. In the afternoon I would have a wash in a barrel of cold water, clean up, put on fresh clothes and go back to London in our own minibus.

The man who was working with me on the bricks had been a hod-carrier for fifteen years. Sometimes he looked tired and would stop for a smoke. I didn't smoke but I waited for him to finish. One day I asked him what age he was and was surprised when he said he was thirty-nine, as I thought he was near fifty. I pondered this for a while. I was twenty-six and I made a conscious decision that I would not spend the rest of my life carrying the hod but I would give it a few more years.

I was also doing part-time bar work in the Crown in Cricklewood. It was a job I really enjoyed as I was off work from the buildings every Saturday and Sunday. The Crown was rough, with more Irish arriving every week. There were plenty of rows and fights and the Black Maria was a common visitor at the main entrance, loading up drunken Irishmen nearly every weekend to take them to the police station. They would have to spend the night there and probably pay a hefty fine the next day for causing a disturbance.

There was an Alsatian dog in the Crown. He generally slept on the floor and did not pass any remarks, even when someone stepped over him. But once a row erupted he would stand on his back legs and let out a ferocious bark. He settled many a row before the police arrived.

Every county in Ireland was well represented in the Crown but Leitrim was very well represented as regards staff. Leitrim was running the bar: men like Peter McGovern, Jack Mulligan, Mickey O'Brien, Val Fitzpatrick, Brendan Shanley, Francie Dillon, Mike Carty, Gerry McGovern, as well as Peter McGovern and myself. Indeed there may have been others from Leitrim that I have forgotten. When a row started, the staff would back each other up and rush to settle it as quickly as possible but it was a dangerous intrusion and many of us were hit with tumblers, kicks and fists. The people who were living in were well protected but the part-time staff members who had to go home after finishing their shift were in danger, as some of the rowdies might be lying in wait in Woolworth's doorway to see if they could recognise the person who had ejected them from the bar. I was one of these part-time barmen who had to face the consequences outside the pub on my way to the Galtymore. I always made sure to make many friends among the customers and when a row blew up, I was reluctant get involved. I'd leave it to the resident bartenders.

I witnessed some fierce fighting on Cricklewood Broadway but never as bad as the night that the Jimmy Shand Scottish Céilí Band played in the Galtymore. The crowd gathered early. The Galty had no licence at this time so many people went out to the Crown to fill up with drink. When they returned the police were manning the door and no one was allowed in or out, even those with passes from a previous visit, as the place was jammed and had been declared a danger. All hell broke loose. The police radioed for backup and a convoy of police vans with Alsatians arrived. At the start the dogs were on leads but then the policemen released them. The people inside were at the windows trying to get a good view of the proceedings. It was even better than Jimmy Shand.

I arrived from my bartending job and had a great view of the goings on but took no part in them. In retrospect, it was an enjoyable night. Some of the dogs got abuse and there was frantic yelping. One Mayo man I knew, who was 6' tall, was attacked by dogs and police. He beat off some of the dogs but about six policemen surrounded him. The Black Maria was parked on a slope thirty yards down the road. The policemen were not very big, maybe about 5' 8". They got hold of the Mayo man and headed him for the Black Maria but every time they got him close to the ramp, he put out his foot and away went the Black Maria, even with the brake on. The crowd was cheering and shouting, the place was bedlam and some missiles were thrown. Finally the policemen got the Mayo man loaded, to the jeers of the onlookers. I'd say he had a sore head the next day.

I was up early the next morning and went to Cricklewood Broadway to buy a paper. The corporation workers were out trying to clean up the mess of the previous night. The headline on the front page of the Sunday paper was: 'Scotchman Jimmy Shand Drives Irish Men Wild on Cricklewood Broadway', accompanied by pictures of the devastation. But in a few weeks all had settled back to normal and there was no more about it.

The Galtymore in Cricklewood was by far the biggest dancing venue for the Irish in London and all the good Irish showbands came to play there, especially in the spring. In Ireland the Catholic Church had banned all dancing during Lent, so these bands were redundant for that period and arranged bookings instead in London, Birmingham, Manchester, New York or wherever they found a venue. For the thousands of Irish emigrants who came to London from the early 1950s to 2008 the Galtymore was more than just a dance hall. It was a home from home, a piece of Ireland, where each weekend they could meet Irish friends from all over London, hear the music from the Irish country and showband scene and, better still, get to meet the showband stars in person.

Celebrations of holidays like St Patrick's Day and Christmas were always special for those who were feeling lonely, exiled and severed from the homeland. It gave people a great boost to meet stars like Larry Cunningham, Dickie Rock, Big Tom and Joe Dolan. The Galtymore was the original ballroom of romance and many a lifelong relationship began there, including my own. Bridie Gallagher, the great Irish ballad singer known as 'the girl from Donegal', made her London début in the Galtymore. Thousands of Irish assembled on Cricklewood Broadway that night, trying to gain admission, and policemen with dogs had to control the crowd and keep a laneway open for passing traffic. The Galtymore was the brainchild of a Kerryman, John Byrne, whom I knew well. And so I should – I danced in the Galty three or four times a week for eight years. John Byrne subsequently returned to Ireland, where he extended his business interests into property and hotels.

Irishmen from all over the country arrived in London in their droves. Some of the men who had arrived in the 1940s had by then become sub-contractors and they could employ who they wished. There were no mechanical diggers at this time: all the work was done by spade and digging fork. If a good, strong young Irishman approached one of these sub-contractors in the pub looking for work, the subby would say, 'Come out in the morning, boots or no boots, and if your mother is a blonde bring her with yeh.' The foreman had a line on the morning the young man started work: 'Go down to the toolbox and get out a pick, you'll work here from eight until a quarter to six, the work it is hard and you might get the sack, and I laughed when he told me I'd never go back.'

The sub-contractors paid £3 a shift (a day) for six days, which came to £18 a week, great money in the mid-1950s. But they paid their workers in the pub on Saturday night, something that involved a lot of drinking. You were one of the hard men now, you could dig muck, you could drink beer with the best of them and the landlady was also Irish. Sunday consisted of two sessions of drinking and some of these hard men were unable to get up for work on Monday mornings. They moved out of the digs about 12 o'clock and headed for the pub again, the only place they knew. At six o'clock the lorry arrived and let off the few men who had made it on the Monday morning. They left a yellow trail of daub from the lorry to the pub. But that did not worry them; they were all tough men with one shoulder up, something that was known as 'the gimp'. The one who missed work that morning were delighted to see his companions again and he apologised to the foreman for not being out that morning because of the rake of beer he had the night before. Then he would buy a round of drinks for the lot. And the foreman said, 'That's all right. You'll be out in the morning.' But what the apologetic labourer did not know was that the sub-contractor did not mind workmen missing Monday. He had booked in so many men with the main contractor and he would be paid anyway. The workmen the sub-contractor did not have to pay but for whom he was paid by the main contractor were known as 'buckshee' workmen.

Men who worked for these sub-contractors were not registered at all in England. They had no national health entitlements or insurance, their cards were not stamped and they paid no tax except what went across the pub counter. So when sickness or retirement age came, they had nothing. The British authorities did not even know they were there. They would have been better off if they had never left Ireland. They are the ones who are talked about today; as 'the forgotten' Irish or the 'homeless' Irish. But these great workmen were not ill-treated by the British. They were screwed by their fellow Irish who ended up as rich developers on the sweat of their countrymen. I know this because as a barman in the Crown, I was part of the Irish diaspora in Britain in the 1950s and I witnessed all this happening before my eyes.

I count myself very lucky that I did not fall into this category of Irish navvy during my time in England. It was easy to get work with these sub-contractors who came from Galway, Mayo, Cork, Kerry, Leitrim or Donegal. They willingly employed their own countrymen and it was lovely to be working with your own people. But apart from the money you might as well be at home, because you never got the opportunity to mix with other nationalities or learn anything except dig muck, drink pints and fight. Of course the landlady with the rake of turnips was from those parts too.

An Irishman in one of these lodging houses was always asking for more meat at the dinner. The landlady got annoyed and said, 'If you eat any more meat that bullock will start lowing inside you.' Paddy replied, 'It won't be for the want of turnips.'

I watched a TV documentary in 2010 called *The Forgotten Irish*. I recognised some of the men, now living in cramped apartments in Camden Town or near the Irish centre, some in poor health and depending on visits from voluntary Irish associations that supply hot dinners or meals on wheels. They worked hard all their lives with one week's pay packet not meeting the next. Most of them had never married and in their own words had no time for the ladies. They reminisced about their childhood years back in Ireland, wondering what it was like over there now, their only connection being a tricolour over the mantelpiece, a picture of the Sacred Heart and a photo of President Kennedy. I even watched one of them return to Tipperary after a fifty-year absence with the help of the Irish Association in London. He did not recognise the homestead or the landscape he had left behind. Finally he made contact with his brother and sister, who were living in the locality but neither of them recognised him and the reunion shown on the television documentary was frosty. So it was back to Camden Town for the rough lay down and the remainder of his days.

The documentary gave the impression that these 'forgotten Irishmen' were the ones who built our country up, sending large sums of money home. This could not be further from the truth. A large proportion of these hard men never had enough money to keep them from one week to the next. They subbed on Monday to get them to Saturday but this was not their fault as they were exploited by their own, the Irish sub-contractors.

16

Work and Play

1958 was a good year for me. I was living on my own in Cricklewood but in no way feeling lonely. I travelled forty miles to Luton every weekday morning to work with the bricklayers and I had part-time work on Saturday and Sunday in the Crown. The Galtymore was just around the corner and I knew a lot of people on Cricklewood Broadway. I ate well, dressed well and drank well. I had money to do all this and surplus. London was becoming like a home from home for me.

One evening when I arrived home from work there was a letter awaiting me, from Val Fitzpatrick, a young man I knew back home in Ireland, who had emigrated to Scotland. He told me that he was coming down to London some time and that he would look me up. He had got my address from my brother Jack.

I threw the letter one side and thought no more of it. The next afternoon when I arrived home, there was Val stretched out on my bed, very comfortable indeed. I looked at him with a stern face and he asked, 'Are you surprised to see me?' I said, 'Yes, but I'm more surprised you wasted the money on the stamp, for you were nearly here before the letter.'

Val and I got on well. We ate our dinner every evening in the Blue Restaurant on Cricklewood Broadway and nearly always chose the same thing: roast pork with apple source, roast potatoes and vegetables. The owner of the restaurant was of Greek origin and he never got to know our names but if he met us outside the restaurant, he would always say, 'Hello, roast pork.' Val got a job as a resident bartender in the Crown and later as a driver on the building site where I was working.

We decided that we would have a good holiday back in Leitrim in the summer of 1958. We arrived home in August; it was a great feeling disembarking from the old narrow-gauge train at Mohill. We secured our luggage in the station and walked up the street. The town itself looked so small, desolate and humble in comparison with the wide streets of London but we had a burning desire to be part of this life once more. We met up with Val's father, Pee, a great character, in Luke Early's and indeed we consumed a consignment of the black stuff. Pee listened to our stories and exploits, most of them exaggerated, then he told us stories about what he'd gone through in his own youth, leaving us feeling very immature indeed.

We had two wonderful weeks' holiday: drinking, dancing and, of course, the girls. Val got the use of his father's Vauxhall Victor, a valuable item of conveyance at the time, and nowhere was too far for us to go. One night we went to see Bridie Gallagher singing in Ballyconnell, County Cavan. Her band was at the top of the music charts with 'The Homes of Donegal'. That was one of the most enjoyable nights of our summer holiday, so good that, later on, unknown to me, Val composed a rhyme about the night. One night, a while after we were back in London, he came to see me and handed me a poem written on an old piece of paper. He said, 'Read that. If you don't like it you can throw it in the fire but remember I've got it anyway.' It has survived fifty-three years and I think, however embarrassing for me, that it's worthy of a place in my life story.

> *The moon was high, the wind was dry,*
> *McGovern combed his hair,*
> *And at half past eight with his thirsty mates,*
> *They started to prepare.*
> *To go to a hop in their old jalopy,*
> *So that they might find the lady,*
> *But first of all, they had to call,*
> *To their good friend, John Eddie Brady.*
>
> *With McGovern's snout well wet with stout,*
> *He said, 'It's time to go.*

It's lovely stuff but I've had enough,
For another hour or so.
So if you start that old tin cart,
To Ballyconnell we'll go.
For I've got to see my girl to be,
She is Miss World, you know.'

Past Solan's store, then Ballinamore,
The Victor roared along.
And every now and then, just like Big Ben,
McGovern gave a song.
Crouched in the back like his brother Jack,
He cracked jokes like a clown,
And at half past ten those boys rolled in.
To that chilly Cavan town.

The place was packed, oh, the walls did crack,
When those boys reached the hall.
For the people came to hear a dame,
Called 'the girl from Donegal'.
McGovern cursed and he said, 'This thirst,
It's time for another drink.
With Guinness's stout I'll cool my drought.
A brainwave – don't you think?'

So out they went because it wasn't lent,
To a wee pub called 'The Log'.
But before we start I've got to part,
To see a man about a dog.
And back he came on to the game,
And he drank a double Scotch.
'We'll now go back and have the craic,
And thank you very much.'

When he arrived he started to jive,
In a most peculiar way.

And McGovern laughed like a man half-daft,
When he sat, I saw him sway.
And then he said in his shoes of suede,
'I'll take one walk through this lot,
And I will view for me and you,
And see what can be got.'

So off he went, hot on the scent,
Until he reached the band.
For it was there he met his former pet,
The girl called Miss Cloudland.
She saw him approach like a lame cockroach,
And she said with a sort of a grin,
'Oh, Andy dear, is it you that's here?
And did they let you in?'

The anthem played, the date was made.
Next Friday is the night.
In Fitz's car we'll travel far,
For I have finished with wheelwright.
Well, there were strange things done
By that son of a gun in the year of '58,
When he drank cheap stout and ran about,
With girls home from the States.

They are gone from him but I'll bet a pin,
And I know that my words are true,
He'll settle down in London town,
A married man, mark you.

Members of the Fitzpatrick family were renowned for their poetry and songwriting so it was no surprise to me when Val presented me with this poem. I was just glad that he did not know more about my life. His uncle, Phil Fitzpatrick, a New York policeman, wrote a song about returning in a dream to his native County Leitrim. 'Lovely Leitrim', became one of the most famous of Irish songs, yet most people do not know who the author was. Phil Fitzpatrick was born in Aughavas in 1892 and emigrated to America in the early 1930s. Tragically, he was killed during a robbery in 1947.

In the early 1960s, Larry Cunningham recorded a new song called 'Among the Wicklow Hills'. On the B-side of that record he put 'Lovely Leitrim'. To his surprise, 'Lovely Leitrim' was the song that made him famous. It was at number one in the Irish charts for sixteen weeks and when Larry Cunningham was invited to the Galtymore in 1964, the like of the crowd that came to see him was never witnessed there before or since. The queue of people trying to gain admission stretched all the way back to Kilburn

With that great holiday of 1958 nearing an end, I decided that I would spend my last Sunday night close to home. I went to a dance in Maguire's hall, only a few hundred yards from my birthplace. I wanted to spend my last night with the boys and girls I had grown up with, school friends, young people with whom I had shared farm work and friends from neighbouring parishes: Cloone, Drumreilly and Carrigallen. I didn't do much dancing that night as I just wanted to talk to these good people as much as possible. I told them how happy I was in London, making good money, and that I was really enjoying life. But, as before, I felt lonely at the thought of leaving home.

I shook off the mantle of sadness and dug deep for my reserves of energy. I would dance and display my so-called happiness. I asked a beautiful girl I had never met before to dance. She was Bridgie Grant, from the parish of Cloone, and we got on very well. She was a good dancer and we talked plenty, so much so that we had a few more dances together. I ended up taking her home that night, all three miles to Cloone, on a bicycle. I told her I was returning to London the next day and that there were no strings attached; we were free to go our separate ways. But we definitely did enjoy each other's company. So what seemed to be a low point in my holiday surprisingly turned out to be an enjoyable evening. I told this girl I might be back at Christmas and that if either of us was involved with someone else that would be okay; we would still be friends and have the occasional dance.

The next day was the end of that summer holiday. I met up with my friend Val Fitzpatrick and once more we boarded the narrow-gauge train at Mohill station. It puffed its way through Derreen bog, sending clouds of white smoke back in the direction of Rosharry. Soon the loneliness disappeared and we joked and laughed all the way to Dublin, Dún Laoghaire, Holyhead and Euston. This journey had become a familiar one for me and it was a saviour when the pockets were empty. It was good to be back in London and to meet up with all my friends from the previous four years. I had paid the rent on my flat and it was nice to get back and not have to go to a notice board looking for accommodation.

The landlord told me that there was someone looking to join me in this accommodation: Mickey Harkins from Granard, County Longford. I knew him well; he was very popular in Cricklewood and the Galtymore, always with a group of girls around him. He was a good worker and kept himself well, not drinking too much but always socialising. He moved in with me and we got on very well. He was a wonderful cook and specialised in cooking legs of lamb, chickens and roast beef, so we had plenty of good, substantial sandwiches to take with us for work. At the weekend we would go out on the town, probably in the company of two girls. If he had any fault it was that he was too popular. We wouldn't be very long in a pub until someone he knew arrived and he would call them over right away. Sometimes we ended up in the company of five or six fellows and their girlfriends. At this time girls did not buy a round but they ordered expensive drinks, such as Tia Maria, vodka, Babycham and gin. I told Mickey that this would have to stop or we would soon run out of money. He laughingly agreed.

One night we were in the Cricklewood Hotel and a row broke out. We were not involved but we knew Ted, the chucker-out, who was having a problem dealing with some of the rowdies. Mickey said to me that we would give Ted a hand. Mickey was small in stature but he could hit a good blow and hold his own with the average man. After some time, with the help of others who knew us well, we got the rowdies out the door, although not without getting a few tattoos ourselves. Mickey laughed his head off about that night and the girlfriends crying, reminiscent of Dominic Behan's line: 'With glasses flying and biddies crying and Paddy going to town'.

On Sundays we headed for the Gaelic grounds at New Eltham. Mickey was a member of the Sean MacDermott club. One Sunday the Sean MacDermotts were playing early in the morning. Mickey was on the team and I went out with them to see the match. They were short some players and Mickey asked me if I would play for them. Of course I togged out and played. Later on in the day the Tara team arrived for a game and I played again with them. Not many recognised me and nobody asked any questions, but it was a stupid thing to do and I could have got both teams suspended. I was probably not much good to either team.

Gaelic football in London was a dangerous game. You could get killed or disabled for life. There were Irish footballers over there who had never kicked a ball at home in their life and they would let out your guts. The Tara team brought out Packie McGarty, one of the best footballers ever to wear a Leitrim jersey, for an important game. Many other counties tried to lure him to play with them but Packie was loyal to Leitrim. Even though he never won many honours with his county team, he always maintained that playing for Leitrim was an honour in itself.

On this particular Sunday he lined out for the Tara team. His brother Willie was the team's manager, director and trainer. The match was with St Mary's, a Kerry combination of immigrants. The teams were well matched and our team was playing well. Packie did not get involved in any of the rough play but kept well on the loose side of the physical tussles. He got a ball that broke at centre field and away he went on a solo run, eluding every attack by the physical backs and delivering the ball to the back of the net.

The St Mary's backs knew that something would have to be done to stop this wizard. Packie relaxed and stayed out of trouble, waiting for the ball to come his way. Off he went again on his solo run, zig-zagging his way through the pouncing Kerry backs. None of them was able to get a hand on him and finally the ball was in the net again. He came out the field, rubbing his hands on his togs, and as he passed by one of the St Mary's backs, the man hit Packie a haymaker

The Tara Gaelic football team that beat St Patrick's, London, in June 1959. Many Leitrim exiles were members, including (back row): Michael Gallagher, Mohill; Raymond Blessing, Aughavas; (centre row): Terry Blessing and Andy McGovern. In the front row (in suit) is Pat Crossan, Ballinamore, with his son, and in the front right corner is Joe McHugh of Fenagh.

of a box straight into the face. Packie fell to the ground, smothered in blood. He was taken to Westminster Hospital and stitched up. He never kicked a ball in London after that and who could blame him. It was suicide playing among those idiots, some of them half-drunk. Packie has a mark on his left cheek to this day. I witnessed this happening, again the Irish abusing their own in a far-off land.

I came home for Christmas of 1958. Construction work in London was off for at least two weeks, depending on the weather, so it was as cheap to go back to Ireland as it was to stay in London. I met up with Bridgie Grant again and we went to a few dances together but at the end of my two weeks of holidays we went our separate ways with no strings attached.

The summer of 1959 was one of the hottest in London for many years, with at least three months of continuous sunshine. I was sunburned black to the waist, as I ran the ladder with my con-signment of bricks. Nobody warned us about melanoma and there was no such thing as sun lotion. Nor was there anyone talking about the ozone layer being punctured. Maybe that sun of fifty years ago was not as harmful as the sun of today.

I was at a dance in the Galtymore one night in 1959, with not a care in the world, when I met Bridgie Grant, the girl from home. We were both delighted to see each other again and I took her home to her apartment that night. She had accommodation in the vicinity of Cricklewood and a job with London Transport as a bus conductor. We agreed to go out together for a while. But as I mentioned with reference to abstaining from meat on a Friday, there were restrictions we abided by. One of the things that was forbidden was living together outside marriage (known then as 'living over the sticks'). We are living in a different world and like having to abstain from meat on Fridays, most of those restrictions are no more. The vast majority of young Irish people living in London in the 1950s and 1960s, no matter which county they came from, were totally committed to the religious teaching of their youth. Whichever part of London one lived in – Cricklewood, Kilburn or Willesden – on a Sunday morning the streets were thronged with Irish men and women going to Mass. They were more anchored to their religion than if they had been at home.

The winter of 1960 was severe, with frost and snow in January, so all construction and building works came to a standstill. It was a hard time for some of the Irish men working with sub-contractors, as they had nothing to fall back on and some had wives and children depending on their weekly wage. I was at Mass in Quex Road, Kilburn, on a Sunday morning about four weeks into this inclement weather when the Irish priest made a generous offer from the pulpit as a gesture to parishioners who were in financial difficulties. He said, 'We have a building fund of £40,000 in the bank. I want any man who has lost his wages to come to the sacristy after Mass and I will pay out £20 per week per workman until this storm is over.' This was a workman's weekly wage at that time. I had never heard of such generosity from any organisation or pulpit. No doubt when the weather improved and everyone was back at work again, the priest and the parish of Quex Road reaped the reward a hundredfold.

Bridgie and I decided to come home on holiday in July 1960. Our two homesteads were only three miles apart and we met each other's parents during this holiday. I hired a car in Longford for the two weeks, which cost me £20, a substantial amount at that time. It was a big car, a Ford Zephyr, and I had never driven a car before. I got a licence in Dublin for £1; anyone could get a licence at this time. When I picked the car up from the car hire firm I told the man I was going to Mohill and he said I would have to turn the car as it was parked the wrong way around. I pretended I had to go to Lanesboro to pick up someone else as I didn't want him to know I couldn't turn the car.

Off we went in the direction of Lanesboro and there were plenty of sudden jumps as I struggled with the gears. At a wide part of the road I slowed down and, as luck would have it, I made the complete turn in one transaction. Now I could negotiate the Mohill road and with every mile I was improving. All went well until we neared Mohill, when we caught up with a removal. This was a tester as I could go fast but not slow; there were plenty of sudden jumps and braking to avoid mounting the car in front. I left Bridgie home and went on to my own place. I got plenty of practice driving that car over the two weeks' holiday.

Back in London, I decided to change my job. I had mastered the task of carrying the hod. My English co-worker was now forty and I could see that he was slowing down. He would stop for a rest and smoke and the rest intervals became more frequent. I encouraged him to take a break, saying that I would carry on working so that the brickies wouldn't catch up with us. But my gut feeling was that I didn't want to be like this man when I was forty.

I had a friend, John Quayne from County Limerick, who was foreman on a building job in Epsom. He offered me work that paid good money so it was goodbye to the hod. The bricklayers were very annoyed that I was leaving but I told them I was finished carrying the hod. I didn't tell them that it was the burned-out man, coughing and trying to get his breath, who had made my mind up for me. So I had a new job and new workmates in a different area of London. John brought me to and from Epsom every day. The work was easy in comparison with carrying the hod. I enjoyed every day I was working with the bricklayers and I was well paid.

At Christmas 1960 Bridgie and I got engaged and we planned to get married the following Easter Monday. This would give us plenty of time to get letters of freedom from our parishes in Ireland. I was still living with Mickey Harkins and life was good, with plenty of socialising. We had two other great friends: John Mulrooney from Ballygar, County Galway, and his wife, Nora O'Connor from Tralee. They had been married a year and had their first child, Liam. They were in the process of buying a house and they offered us their apartment, consisting of two bedrooms, a kitchen and a bathroom. There were no other tenants in the house, just the owner and his wife, both elderly. It was right beside Cricklewood Broadway, very convenient to the bus station where Bridgie was working and the Galtymore, also to the Crown where I was still doing some part-time bartending. So far so good: Bridgie would move into the apartment when it became vacant and I would move in after the wedding.

17

Tying the Knot

On Easter Monday, 3 April 1961, Bridgie and I were married in St Agnes's, Cricklewood Lane, the church I had attended for the previous six years. The reception was in the Robin Hood Hotel in Harleston and it was a wonderful day of celebration for all our friends. My brother, Jack, came over from home to be best man and Val Fitzpatrick also made the trip from Ireland.

That summer we returned to Ireland on holiday to celebrate our marriage with our parents and our many friends in Aughavas

The wedding day of Andy McGovern and Bridgie Grant.

and Cloone. Bridgie discovered that she was pregnant with our
first child, another cause for celebration. Going into marriage we
discussed having children and decided: whatever will be, will be.
Again, our upbringing determined the future, as we left it up to
God. Once we had made the decision we were happy and looked
forward to this special event. Later that year Bridgie had to give up
her job as a bus conductor. I had a good job and part-time work in
the Crown, so there were no financial problems whatsoever. As a
matter of fact I looked forward to coming home from work in the
evening and finding a nice warm house and a lovely dinner awaiting
me. It reminded me of my ploughing days back in Corroneary, with
my mother always at home.

Christmas of 1961 was lovely for both of us, as we awaited the
birth of our firstborn. We did not mind whether it was a boy or a
girl as long as the child was in good health; nor did we discuss any
names. Bridgie attended Kingsbury Maternity Hospital on a weekly
basis and all reports were that mother and baby were healthy. The
hospital was some distance from us but the underground train
service was good on the Bakerloo line. I was still working out in
Epsom, a long journey from Cricklewood. On the afternoon of 1
February 1962, I came home and discovered a note Bridgie had left
for me: she was going to Kingsbury as she was in some discomfort.

The phone service then was nothing like it is today. There was
no phone in our house and very bad service from the local call box
so I decided I would clean up and go to the hospital. When I arrived
I found Bridgie in great shape, relaxed and in good humour. The
hospital staff assured me that there was no need for panic, that they
were holding her for observation and that the birth could be days
away. It was a relief to know that mother and baby were safe in the
hands of the professionals. Bridgie told me to go home and go to
work the next day and give a ring about dinner time.

The next morning I went to work out in Epsom but I was very
edgy and fidgety and couldn't concentrate on what I was doing. We
always got a ten o'clock tea break and I couldn't wait any longer, so
I headed for the nearest telephone kiosk. I dialled the hospital and
give my name and particulars and the nurse asked me to hold on a

minute. It was the longest minute I was ever on a phone. When she came back she said, 'Mr McGovern, your wife Bridget give birth to a beautiful baby boy this morning. They are both doing fine.' I felt like saying, 'What about me?' but I don't remember what I did say, nor do I remember thanking the nurse. I stood in that kiosk for some time, shaking, with tears of joy trickling down my Irish cheeks.

I felt like cheering and shouting at the top of my voice but I didn't want to attract the attention of those who would consider me 'another Irishman gone berserk'. I walked slowly back to the construction site and knew that my life would never be the same again. I had a profound responsibility to provide for my wife, my son and any other children we might have. When I got back to the site I decided that I would not tell any of my workmates my news. This was my celebration and I was not going to let it become a joke, or listen to any smart or derogatory remarks about it. My friend, the boss, approached me privately and I told him the good news. He said I should go home and go to see Bridgie and the new baby. 'Anyway,' he said, 'you're not going to be any good to me in your present condition.'

So I started for Cricklewood. It was a long train journey with several changes but soon I was on my way to Kingsbury Hospital with my bouquet of flowers. I felt like singing the line from the song, 'My feet ain't touching the ground.' Bridgie looked terrific, beaming with happiness, and there were also a few tears in our greeting. Words deserted us and Bridgie beckoned to the nurse to bring in the baby. The nurse wheeled in a little cot with the most beautiful baby I had ever seen, with a lovely head of dark hair, just as I had when I was his age. And, yes, I did see a likeness of me in this baby, although I didn't say it because I knew it was the mother who had done most of the hard work. The nurse reached into the cot to lift the child, saying, 'Come on, Andy, turn around here till we see you.' Well, I got the shock of my life; at first I thought she was talking to me. Bridgie explained that when they were taking the baby into the nursery it was important to have a name tag on its wrist. When the nurse asked Bridgie the name she should put on it, Bridgie replied, 'What name but the father's? He's the image of him.' And Andy it was.

In a few days' time, Bridgie was home with our little bundle of joy. It it hard to imagine that a helpless little child could make so much work. Every move he made and every breath he took we were watching him. If he cried at night, one of us was out of the bed in a shot. We had five other children but none of them seemed to cause as much work as the first. In two weeks the baby was christened, as our religion decreed. Nora Mulrooney was godmother and Gerry McGovern godfather. We had a wonderful day and whether it was the parents who had settled or the child, things did improve and there was definitely less crying at night.

I was still working out in Epsom and bartending all the time I could get. There was now a strain on our financial resources and socialising was almost a thing of the past. But the little man was so interesting that I forgot about such things. Every week there was a new development: a smile, a laugh; trying to get on his hands and knees – oh, yes, we recorded everything in our memories. That winter, Bridgie decided that she would go back to work. We got a good child-minder just across the road from us, even though we were reluctant to part with our little man.

Christmas of 1962 was severe, yet again, and construction work came to a halt. Bridgie had to go down to Chiswick, to the head-quarters of London Transport, to collect her uniform and report for work as bus conductor. I was doing nothing that day so she asked me to come along with her. While I was waiting for her to finish with her business, I saw a sign in the station: 'Cable Hand Wanted'. I went over to the desk and asked about the job and I was handed some papers and told to fill them in.

To my surprise I was called into another section and promised the job as a cable hand but first of all I had to wait for a doctor to come to give me a medical examination. About six hours after my first enquiry, I was offered the job. The pay wasn't great but the job had some interesting fringe benefits, such as free travel in London and free travel to Ireland once a year. It had a pension fund and pro-vision for sick pay. I would be working in Neasden, not far from where we lived. So it was goodbye to construction work.

I was fascinated by my new-found job or maybe the truth is that

I was bored. I had been a physical worker all my life and enjoyed being active but this was the laziest job you could imagine. It went something like this: I clocked in at eight o'clock. There were five in our gang, including the charge hand, and we each had our own locker, with uniform and working clothes. The charge hand approached the manager at nine o'clock to get a schedule of our work for the day. Then we had tea and fairy cakes before setting out for the underground station involved. We had to give priority to the passengers using the underground transport, as these people paid our wages.

When we arrived at the station, we would find that a cable carrying the current had been closed down and replaced by a substitute cable. Our job was to repair this cable. With two of us working and three looking on, it took about an hour. It was then time for more tea in the canteen. We gathered up the tools and admired the new joint we had secured in a lead mould and went back to headquarters at Neasden. We changed our clothes, stowed our uniform in the locker, washed up and that was the end of work for the day. By then it was four o'clock and we had to wait until five o'clock to clock out. There was only one thing to do: more tea and fairy cakes. Sometime we played cards. The workforce was drawn from different nationalities but we were all loyal to London Transport.

For the first few weeks of my employment I thought I would not be able to stick the boredom but after six months I was just like the rest of them, complaining about all the work we were doing. Every month we had to do a week on nights, which was even worse. At about midnight we got the last train to wherever a job had to be done; the current and all trains were off until six in the morning. Sometimes if we were working near home and finished early, we walked the underground tunnel to go home, with one person designated to get back to the station and clock the others out at eight o'clock.

In the summer of 1963, Bridgie and I returned home on holiday to show off our offspring. We had a wonderful time. No matter how good London was as regards work and money, I was still anchored to the homeland. That September Bridgie discovered that she was pregnant again. We were delighted at the thought of a comrade for our little man and we would no more have thought of using contra- ceptives than eaten meat on Friday. But this second pregnancy forced us to make a decision about our future life. We had two options: stay in London and bring up our children as English, or return to Ireland and give them an Irish formation. We wrestled with the decision for some time. Finally we decided we would return to live in Ireland in the spring of 1964. Our second child was due in May.

18

Goodbye to London

I gave up my job with London Transport and we vacated our comfortable apartment. A man from Mohill, Jerry Diffley, moved into our apartment. We returned to Ireland in February 1964 and severed our ties with London. We rented accommodation and I got a job as a lorry driver with a local company for a wage of £14 a week, half what I was getting with London Transport.

The work was tough and dangerous at times because of the condition of the lorry. Sometimes I left for Dublin at seven in the morning and drew rails all day from the North Wall to Clondalkin. The last load would be for Mohill, a hundred miles away. I often thought of my relaxed colleagues in London Transport having cups of tea and fairy cakes.

On 3 May our second baby was born in Nurse Maguire's nursing home in Longford. He was a beautiful boy with curly fair hair and we christened him Raymond. We could not survive on my low income and, as the sole provider, I was no longer willing to risk my life in the old lorry. I heard of a job going in Wales, not far from Holyhead, and thought I would try it out, although I hated being parted from my little family. On a Sunday afternoon I arrived in Wales and enquired about the project, a nuclear power station that was just starting at Wylfa, eighteen miles from Holyhead. I got a bus out there late that afternoon.

The site was enormous, with living accommodation for the workers. I had a case and a toolbox. I approached the security man on the gate and he said, 'They're crying out for chippies [carpenters] here.' I felt like replying, 'They'll be crying when they get this one.' He directed me to an office where I could book in for free accommodation for the night. He also showed me where the canteen was and told me where to go in the morning to get a job.

The next morning I went down to the labour office. There were about fifteen men outside, all looking for work. A big specimen of a man came to the door of the office and shouted, 'Any chippies here?' I stepped forward, along with another man I didn't know. We went into the office and presented our cards and were employed right away. He told us to go to the pump house that was being constructed and that our work would involve shuttering, something I did understand. My new friend, Brian Roddy, was English, of Irish parents, and while we were on our way to the pump house, he asked me if we could stay together as a team. I told him I would be delighted. He half-smiled and said, 'I don't know much about this work, I've just come out of the army.' 'Well,' I said, 'that makes two of us who know nothing. I was depending on you.' We both laughed and I said, 'We'll muddle our way through it.'

The pump house was an enormous building, where the water was brought in from the sea to be used to cool the reactors when the nuclear power station was complete. A big foreman approached us, welcomed us and said that he was sorry to have to break us up for a few weeks, explaining that he was a man short in two different gangs. He promised that he would put us together again. We didn't complain as we knew it could be a blessing in disguise.

He asked us where we came from, wrote out a note and said that if we went to the money office we would be refunded the money for our fares to get there. I was in a gang of about four chippies and the job was easy to learn. A crane lifted the big shutters and put them in position for the next pour of concrete. The walls were about six foot wide and all we had to do was plumb the shutter down to the datum at the foundation (the level from which measurements are taken) and stabilise it to the specified instructions. An engineer inspected the work before the concrete was poured so the responsibility was his.

It was one of the best jobs I ever had in England, paying about £50 a week, four times as much as the company at home with its outdated lorry. If there was a downside to the job, it was being away from home but the company, Taylor Woodrow, gave us a break every six weeks and paid our fare home, also paying us wages for the Monday of our return. They supplied transport to and from Holyhead. I could leave Mohill at four o'clock on a Monday afternoon and be in bed on the site at one in the morning as it was direct transport all the way.

Brian Roddy and I shared a nicely kept room with two beds: there were two workmen to every room. Cleaners maintained the rooms and all meals were supplied in the canteen but we bought an electric kettle so that we could have a cup of tea at night. We discussed the work we were both now learning, trying to help each other along. We were two chancers and got many a good laugh out of it. That was the thing about working in the UK: if you could do the job, there were no questions asked. The work we did one week was repeated the following week as those massive shutters were put into position for another concrete pour. There were three other so-called chippies from Leitrim: Ted Gaffney, Drumsna; Jim Gilhooly, Drumshambo; and Pat Conboy, Aughavas. They are all deceased, RIP, while I have survived, against the odds, as you already know.

We worked twelve consecutive days, then had the following Saturday and Sunday off. We were paid double time for the Saturday and Sunday we worked and we would gladly have worked every Saturday and Sunday if we were let. This new power station was situated in a wilderness and, although there were licensed premises on the site, it wasn't the same as drinking on a night out. I just wanted to work and look forward to returning to my lovely little family every six weeks with plenty of money and gifts.

The firm proposed that we do three weeks' continuous work in the run-up to Christmas 1964, so that we would have extra money for the holidays. But the union objected, telling us that the firm was only using us, and the issue was to be put to an all-out vote in the car park the following day. There were a lot of local people employed on this site, as well as workers bussed in from other districts. They wanted the employment to continue as long as possible as it was the first time they had experienced such wages.

The meeting in the car park was rough, with the union bosses telling the firm in no uncertain manner where to stick their overtime.

When the vote was taken, it was clear that the locals had rejected the firm's proposition and the workers living on the site had to refrain from working the Saturday and Sunday before Christmas.

As I lay in bed on the Saturday and Sunday mornings, I thought about what the unions were doing to some of their members. I appreciated the great work they had done, releasing workers from the chains of slave labour. But I also wondered: how far can one go? You can bend a rod but if you bend it too much it will break. As I write, big firms such as Taylor Woodrow, McAlpine, Wimpey, John Laing and Unit Construction are no longer employing direct labour in the way they used to, simply because they could not satisfy the unions' demands. These firms now sublet their work to sub-contractors and where does the worker end up? Worse off than before: more work for less money and poorer conditions. I can see the same happening here in Ireland, where our large companies are setting their work out to agencies (a nice word for sub-contractors) because they cannot meet the demands of unions. For example, state-run nursing homes are being closed and private nursing homes are taking over, with fewer nurses and more domestic staff. Just as happened in England, we broke the rod.

19

Building Our Dream

I worked on in Wales until the summer of 1965, coming home every six weeks, although I knew that this divided family was not the way we had planned to live. It was a terrible strain on all of us but the money did go some way towards compensating for it. That summer Bridgie's parents, who were getting on in life, signed over their farm to us. It was a small farm but it was a base and we were grateful to inherit it. Our children were our priority, as we both yearned for them to experience the joys of being reared in the Irish countryside, to be free as birds to run down hillsides with the wind in their hair, to seek out frogs in ponds, to watch little rabbits at play, to experience the delight of holding a day-old chick in their hands, to enjoy the simple pleasures of country life as we both had.

On 26 September our first daughter was born. She was a beautiful baby with dark hair and was greatly welcomed into the family. There was plenty of work to be done, stocking up the farm, and we also needed a new house. We were young, strong and healthy and nothing would could stop us pursuing our dream. We bought some cows, milked them by hand and sent their milk to the creamery. It was lovely work and the animals were very contented in comparison with the cows of today. One lovely summer's day stands out in my memory. We were busy saving the hay. We worked late with some of the children propped up in the meadow, free and safe with that beautiful rich smell of fresh hay. The cows were lowing at the gateway to the pastures for someone to milk them. We secured the children, then approached the cows with two small stools and the milking vessels and started to milk them where they stood in the field. It was like a competition as the animals greeted us with wondrous looks, as if to say, 'Is it me, is it me, or is it me?'

Our young hearts were bursting with happiness. We rose early in the morning and retired late at night and our days were filled with hard work. When it is a labour of love, the shoulders carry the weight with ease. The determination to make our dream come true gave us tremendous strength.

No artificial manure was used on pastureland at this time and we definitely gave no meal to the cows, yet their milk overflowed our buckets. They were small cows – cross Angus, Hereford and Shorthorn – compared to the continental breeds of today. But today's cows have no milk in comparison; they get it hard to feed their calf. They get meal and the calf gets meal and the land gets artificial manure and has plenty of grass so I can't understand why these big cows cannot fill a bucket of milk.

Slowly a little crack began to appear in our dream, with the realisation that it was impossible to make a living for a family on a small farm in County Leitrim in the 1960s. The few pounds we had saved were dwindling fast as we bought the necessary equipment: a car, a tractor and other machinery. I got part-time work operating machinery for different contractors: Paddy Nicholl, Rossan; Sadie McGovern, Ballinamore; Paddy McManus, Drumshambo; and Danny McGee, Gortlettra. The wages were modest but at least I was getting experience of driving mechanical diggers and bulldozers.

I was fairly good at this work so in 1968 I decided to buy my own machine. I was entering into the unknown and for the first time in my life I had to borrow some money to get started. I went to Tractamotors, Cavan, to view some machines they had brought in from England. I chose a JCB 3C, one of the first machines turned out by Joseph Cecil Bamford. It was a very strong machine, the first of its kind in Cloone or Aughavas, and I secured a contract to dig a two-mile group water scheme in Aughavas, a small job but a start. This was 1969 and it was hard to believe how little Ireland had moved since my childhood in the 1940s. There was no running water in any of the rural houses, no baths, showers or flush toilets. The group water scheme was the solution. The government of the day was prepared to subsidise these schemes, whereby two or more householders got together to provide themselves with a water supply either from the mains or a private source. I was delighted to be involved in improving the standard of living of the local people.

In 1968 Leitrim County Council employed a public-health inspector named Terence McHugh to inspect the water supply to the village of Cloone and the surrounding areas. He discovered that the only water supply was from local wells: Scott's well on the Ballinamore road and McCabe's well in Esker. There was also a hand-pumped well in Pope's yard and another at the parish priest's house but the quality of their water was poor. People got their domestic water supply from rooftops, collected into barrels and concrete tanks.

The health inspector was convinced that a group water scheme should be established in the parish of Cloone. He set about testing water in various lakes in the surrounding districts and discovered a lake within the drumlin hills of Adoon and Gorvagh, three-and-a-half miles from Cloone, with a high quality of drinking water. There were very few residents and little farming in the vicinity of this lake so effluent or contamination wouldn't be a problem. He established that a hill a quarter of a mile from the lake would be an ideal place for a reservoir and that this reservoir would have sufficient height to

Andy with his JCB at the start of the Cloone group water scheme in 1968.

supply most of the parish of Cloone with a first-class water system.

Terence McHugh approached Peter Charles, then a county councillor, with this proposition. Good grants were available from government and local government. McHugh made numerous trips to Cloone to try to get the scheme started and Peter Charles agreed to form a local committee, involving people whose consent was needed to build the reservoir and construct the pump house and to grant access to the lake and the main road. There were numerous meetings at which the inspector explained his plans.

The committee comprised: Peter Charles, Gabriel Moran, John Kelly, P. Joe Heeran RIP, Paddy Beirne RIP, Mike Joe Brennan RIP, Paddy Quinn RIP, Patsy McGowan RIP and Sean Dillon RIP. Those men worked in harmony to move the project forward and the county council appointed an engineer, Trevor MacDonald RIP, to oversee the project. He visited Cloone each week to inspect the work.

The wheels were now set in motion. P. Joe Heeran consented to the reservoir being erected on his land and allowed access to the pump house and roadway. Thomas McKeon RIP, Adoon, give permission for the pipeline to cross his lands. A pump house was erected close to the lake and, four feet from the lake shore, one could look down twelve feet into clear, blue, spring water, a sight to behold. The reservoir, with a total capacity of 100,000 gallons, was erected by Mercers Solon, Precast Construction Ltd, Mullingar, and a three-inch pipeline was installed, complete with electric cable from the pump house to the reservoir. A float switch on the inside of the reservoir determined when the pump would cut in or out. Everything worked perfectly.

Many workers gave their time and labour free to transport materials to the reservoir. Owen and Sean Mitchell participated in this voluntary work and gave permission for access to the lake and the reservoir.

It was then time to lay the water mains. Wavin Plastic, Balbriggan, was the supplier of the plastic piping and other materials. The plastic pipes were in twenty-foot lengths, joined by a simple plastic collar with two rubber 'O' rings sealing the joint, and these materials was guaranteed for twenty years. I was fortunate to secure the contract for the excavation and the laying of the mains pipeline. Work started in November 1969, when the first three-inch mains pipes were laid. By Christmas that year, the pipeline was complete as far as the village of Cloone. Mike Joe Brennan and Patsy McGowan were responsible for all house connections. The committee set a charge of £40 per household, which included a half-inch water tap to each kitchen and a ceramic sink. Some people opted to instal modern stainless steel sinks instead. Decades later, ceramic sinks became fashionable again.

I employed one workman, John McKiernan, who resigned at Christmas 1969 because of family commitments. William McLoughlin RIP was then my only employee until the project was completed. There were many extensions to the scheme that was originally planned, including one to Annaghmacullen. Michael Kelleher, Pee Rourke RIP and Pat Frank Lyons RIP were the instigators of this two-and-a-half mile extension. Michael Kelleher was chairperson and had to persuade households living in proximity to the extension to become part of the scheme, explaining to them that a council water supply would not come their way for years. How right he was.

By 1972, twenty miles of water mains had been completed and a hundred homes connected. There was no charge for or restrictions on water use and this proved to be an error of judgment. Water waste was rampant, with taps left running and burst pipes and leaks not reported. The pump was working full-time and soon had to be replaced. Twenty years later, the water in the lake was re-tested and found to be contaminated, so the county council agreed to supply a connection to the reservoir from their mains pipeline on the road between Mohall and Ballinamore.

This solved the problem for a time but soon the council discovered that they could not keep up with the demand for water. A meeting was held and it was agreed that meters would have to be installed in every house connection. Each house would be allocated a specified number of gallons of water free and thereafter a charge would be applied. This system worked very well. All the house connections were checked and repaired and householders also checked their own lines in case they were charged for any waste water. The scheme is now working effectively. Much credit is due to the three members – Michael Kelleher, Gabriel Moran and John Kelly – who report, repair and keep a watchful eye, ensuring that there is no waste or abuse of the scheme. Packie Joe McGarry also deserves praise for his great work over the years in repairing damaged pipes and leaks.

It is amazing how this water scheme has survived for forty-three years, with a little rubber 'O' ring holding back the pressure every twenty feet of mains pipeline. As I write, a hundred-and-eighty-six households are connected to this scheme. How many of these householders spare a thought or a prayer for the gallant group that had the foresight to start this water scheme forty-three years ago, so that the people of Cloone would no longer have to haul buckets of water from lakes, rivers or spring wells?

The group water scheme in Cloone set a precedent and thereafter I seemed to win every contract I tendered for: Gorvagh, Ohill, Leitrim village, Cootehall, Drumsna, Newtowngore, Derrycasson, Levereen, Aughavas and Aughancliff. We used the money I earned from these contracts to build our new house without having to take out a loan or mortgage. The work on the house would slow down until the cheque from the water works arrived; it was as simple as that. I had inherited a fear of borrowing from my parents and they in turn from their parents, who lived in an era when not being able to pay meant eviction.

I remember hearing an interview on Shannonside Radio with the great musician Paddy Cole, then in his eighties, about his youth in County Monaghan. If you wanted an item such as a table or chair, or wanted to replace an old bed, you had to wait until you had the money. He remembered the bed going with the daughter who had just got married. He questioned today's way of thinking: people who borrow as if there is no tomorrow, build a new home with all modern conveniences, an en-suite in every bedroom and a fitted kitchen better than anyone else's and then go to Spain on holiday.

In 1975, for the first time in our married life, we seemed to be on a firm footing. By then we had six beautiful, healthy children, four girls and two boys. Anita was born in 1967, Sheila in 1971 and Pauline in 1974. The family was complete. We had inherited my parents' thirty-acre farm at Corroneary and the Land Commission allocated us more land in Sunnamore. As far as land was concerned, we had enough. I built up a herd of suckling cows and sold their calves at the age of six to nine months. This provided a good income and demanded very little work and there was a Department of Agricultural heritage payment on the stock. The water scheme contracts and the income from the farm made us fairly secure. Lady Luck was smiling down on us. As the proverb says, 'It's tomorrow we know how happy we were yesterday.'

There was increasing demand for me to take on water schemes. I contemplated buying more machinery and employing more work-men but I hesitated, as it would create a lot of extra responsibility for me, as well as involving borrowing money. How would I get a driver who would care for a machine as if it were his own? When the water scheme was completed, I would be the one responsible for its success but I couldn't be in two places at the one time. So I decided to stick with the one machine and do what I could. It was the best decision I ever made.

Brucellosis become rampant among the herds of cattle in our area, causing in-calf cows to abort their calves before the birth was due. I had a compulsory herd test which proved that four of my cows had this disease. They had to be sent to the factory for slaughter. There months later, I had another test and seven cows were found to have the disease. The adviser from the Department of Agriculture recommended that I have the entire herd removed and slaughtered. It was a highly contagious disease and eventually all female stock would be infected.

It was a very hard decision. A week later the lorry arrived and with sinking hearts we watched our twenty choice cows being hushed up the ramp. We shed tears for the cows whose lives were now being cut short and their unborn calves that were to be our future. With sinking hearts, we walked the empty fields and viewed the silent sheds. The mornings were hushed, the lowing of cows a distant memory. We had come from the purchase of one cow a few years previously to building up this fine herd, something I had dreamed about in my youth. Now, with the stroke of a pen, all was lost. Yes, there was compensation but how can one be compensated for the emotional loss? No price can ever be put on a shattered dream.

The adviser from the Department of Agriculture told me it would be all right to buy bullocks or other male cattle, which were not affected by brucellosis, but I didn't have the heart to invest in new livestock at this time. I continued with my JCB and the water schemes.

20

The Diagnosis

In 1976, Bridgie got a severe pain in her right arm. Her GP referred her to St Vincent's Hospital, Dublin. I took her there and had to enquire the way. She was diagnosed with carpal tunnel syndrome, something to do with a trapped sinew in her wrist. She had a small operation and everything was fine again. The same year, while stretching out my right arm, I discovered that one finger had dropped down. It was unable to resist the pull of gravity, no matter how I tried to bring the finger up flush with the other four fingers. I just laughed at this inadequacy. There was no pain and it did not affect my work in any way. With hindsight, I can see how we were oblivious to the disaster clouds that were slowly moving in our direction.

Later that year I was shaving in the bathroom one Saturday night. I had the razor in my hand but was unable to reach up to my jaw. I hesitated and looked down, as I thought one of the small children was tugging my arm. But there was no one there. I changed the razor to a different grip in my hand and everything was okay. Again, I laughed at this occurrence.

Bridgie got arthritis and after some x-rays, she was told that she would have to have a hip replacement. At the end of 1976, my mother became very ill and we sat up with her at night. She died on 3 January 1977. May she rest in peace

One night my brother Jack handed me a glass of Guinness and I had to struggle to keep the glass from turning upside down in my hand. I changed my grip and succeeded in drinking from the glass, a bit awkwardly. We did talk about my problem that night. I knew that something was definitely wrong with my hand and arm. Soon I found another finger dropping, like the one that was already down.

I didn't think it was anything to get excited about but I did go to my GP, Enda Cadden of Mohill. He told me I had a nerve problem and that whatever about arresting it there would be no such thing as reversing it. He referred me to a specialist at St Vincent's. This time I did not have to enquire the way. I was admitted and the tests began. Every test came back negative. After six weeks one of the specialists said to me, 'I can't find anything wrong with you. You are in a perfect state of health. But I'm not saying that there might not be something the matter, so I'm referring you to a neurologist.' Next morning, Professor Eddie Martin came to visit me. He examined me briefly and walked me up and down the ward in my underpants. Dr Martin said, 'We have a lot more tests to do on you, starting to-morrow morning.' I had more blood tests, a spine scan, a brain scan and muscle biopsies.

I got very frustrated because I was so long in hospital. My wife was busy looking after the children and the cattle so I wrote to her, as we had no phone at home, and told her not to come up to Dublin, that I was in good health and that the most important thing was to mind the children. One morning I asked Dr Martin when he would be able to give me a diagnosis. He said that there was another neuro-logist taking up a position in St Vincent's that week and that he would like this specialist to look at my test results. Between them they would have a diagnosis the following Friday and I would be able to go home. This was music to my ears, as work was piling up at home and my JCB was standing idle.

On the Friday morning, the two specialists came to see me with arms full of papers and files. Dr Martin introduced me to Dr Michael Hutchinson, a young, fresh, man from Northern Ireland, who greeted me with a handshake. Dr Martin said, 'Dr Hutchinson and I have been looking at your files and all your tests and we have come to a joint diagnosis of your condition. We are certain that you have motor neurone disease. We are putting you on a course of injections to be administered by your own GP and we will be calling you back in a few weeks' time, to monitor the progress of this disease. As yet there is no cure for this disease but we are opti-mistic that research will soon come up with something to at least arrest it. You can go home today.' I asked no questions. As far as I was concerned motor neurone disease was like algebra: I had never heard of it. All I wanted was to get out of that hospital and back to my loving family and my JCB.

I arrived home in great humour. At least I had an answer. Many tests for various diseases and illness had proven negative. I was a healthy man, or so I was told. One night as the family was watching TV, a man name Stephen Hawking appeared on the screen in a wheelchair, talking about his illness. My ten-year-old daughter said, 'Daddy, that's what you've got.' 'No,' I said, 'that man is in a wheelchair.' My daughter repeated that the man on the screen had said he had motor neurone disease. The atmosphere changed completely and there was silence in the kitchen. My other children stared at my outspoken daughter and she made her exit from the gathering. I wondered if my family knew more than I did.

At my next outpatient's appointment at Dr Hutchinson's clinic, I was determined to ask more questions. I was called into a room and three or four doctors (perhaps including one or two students) examined me. I asked them about the disease but did not get a satisfactory answer. One of them said, 'Ask Big Chief when he comes in,' referring to Dr Hutchinson. When Dr Hutchinson arrived, he had a tremendous welcome for me, heartily shaking my hand. But I knew that by doing this he was also estimating the gravity of the loss of power in my hand and arm. 'You're doing well,' he said. I asked him about the seriousness of the disease. He took a deep breath and become sombre. 'Yes, Andy,' he said. 'The prognosis with this disease is not good. The life expectancy is between two and five years but you are a very fit man and I would be surprised if you did not get much longer than that. We will keep your condition monitored but there's no treatment for it yet. Scientists and researchers are working hard all over the world to find a cure for this disease and we are expecting a breakthrough soon.'

The time for denial was over. This was reality. How long did I have? Six years was nothing in comparison with the future I had planned. I had to adopt two personalities: one to deal with the feeling that was eating me up, the 'why me' syndrome, and the other to pretend to my wife and children that I was reasonably happy with my condition. As I drove home the faces of my six children kept appearing before me. What lay ahead for them? Who would care for them? Would I be there to see them grow up? I worried for my wife, Bridgie. How would she cope alone? Her health was not the best. Would she be able to manage the children and the farm? I was distressed, alone and helpless. I knew nobody with this disease, I had no access to information about it and in my heart I suppose I did not really want this information.

Back home, I had a few water scheme contracts to complete. I stood on the back of the digger with my arms down. I had no problem operating the machine but if a pipe burst or any mainten-ance work had to be done on the digger my hand was useless. I would have to get one of my sons to put the wrench on a nut so that I could turn it. The lean-down strength of my arm was still good but I was finding it hard to eat a sandwich or lift a mug of tea to my mouth. Indeed, many days I fasted until I got home, for fear that someone would see me struggling with my condition.

My right arm got weaker and weaker. Feeding utensils started falling out of my hand. I would knock a cup of tea all over myself and my piece of meat or potato would go for my ear instead of my mouth. My coordination was all askew. Even taking up a glass of Guinness was a thing of the past. I became angry, bitter, frustrated and embarrassed and all the time I was thinking of the doctor's sentence: two to six years and mortality.

Bridgie was called to Cappagh Orthopaedic Hospital for her hip replacement. I drove her up and visited her many times, always bringing some of the children with me. I could drive the car with my one good hand but I could not turn the key in the ignition and if I had to change a wheel I needed the assistance of some of the children. Bridgie made a wonderful recovery. In 1979, I had com-pleted all outstanding contracts and I refused to take on others, although I was still trying to conceal my illness. I used the digger as an excuse, telling people that it was nearly finished. But the digger won the battle; it was I who was nearly finished. Good old JCB, hard to subdue. I built up a herd of cows again to give me an interest in some farm work and take my mind off the inevitable prognosis.

At this, my lowest point in coming to terms with my disease, I received a demand from the Revenue Commissioners for £3500 that they claimed I owed them. This was the way the Revenue did business: they estimated a figure and it was up to you to prove that you did not owe the amount. I would have to employ a solicitor to defend this demand. I did not reply to the letter but soon another one arrived, I ignored it and another one arrived. I was told that this would be the last notification before court proceedings were instituted. I studied the tax form and noticed a line that read, 'If you need any help filling this form do not hesitate to get in touch with us and our representative will visit you and help you with it.' I wrote a brief note to the tax office saying that I did need help completing the form.

A week later an official from the Revenue Commissioners arrived. He needed no introduction as his briefcase and moustache were an adequate representation of his position. I welcomed him into the house, treating him with great courtesy. He produced receipts of money I had received since 1969, evidence of various contracts I had carried out. At one stage he pointed out that the Revenue was going light on me and that there would be no reduction in the amount I would have to pay. At that moment, four of the children came in from primary school. I asked him if the Revenue had taken them into consideration. He enquired how many children we had and I said six under the age of fifteen. He twirled his pen and said, 'There might be a small reduction but I mean a very small reduction. You are a well-established contractor.'

I replied that I wouldn't be a contractor any longer. I told him I'd just been diagnosed with a terminal condition, motor neurone disease. He dropped the pen, looked at me over his dark-rimmed glasses and asked, 'Have you any medical proof of this?' I produced my doctor's letter and said to him, 'If that's not proof enough for you, take a look at the muscles wasting in my hand and arm.' Bridgie offered him a cup of tea and he accepted gratefully. There was very little talk coming from him until he said, 'I had a good friend who died from that disease a few years ago. One thing I can tell you for sure is that you will never hear about this tax liability again.' He wrote something on the tax form, folded up his papers, shook hands with both of us and wished us well. I thanked him profusely and he was on his way. We didn't hear anything more from the Revenue.

As the disease progressed, my arm got weaker and weaker and I found myself hiding away and avoiding meeting people. My social life was a no-go area and I hibernated within the family circle. I used the children to cover up for my inadequacies. If I visited the homes of relatives, I would bring one or more of the children with me and I wouldn't take refreshments in any house. When we were leaving for home, if some of the people from the house came as far as the car, I would nudge the child with my knee to remind him or her to turn the key in the ignition. The children were good at protecting me from embarrassment. They were drivers before their time.

Bridgie's arthritis continued to spread; soon she would have to have the other hip replaced. She had still not reached forty and I was forty-five. Some weeks we made three visits to St Vincent's, as Bridgie and I had appointments with different doctors at different times.

Dr Hutchinson referred me for a second opinion to a neuro-logist in the Richmond Hospital and I drove up one morning for my appointment, bringing my twelve-year-old daughter with me in case anything went wrong. A nurse showed me into a cubicle and asked me to strip off down to my underpants. Soon the neurologist arrived. He enquired who had sent me there and asked what my diagnosis had been in St Vincent's. When I replied, 'motor neurone disease,' he said, 'That's what you have; I can see the fasciculation [twitching] in your stomach muscles. Put on your clothes. I can do nothing for you and nobody else can either. Go home and put your affairs in order.'

I had never felt so low and angry in all my life. How could I tell my young daughter what the doctor had said, while concentrating on driving a hundred miles to Leitrim with one hand. Thank God there is now counselling, as well as emotional support, for people newly diagnosed with motor neurone disease.

Our financial resources were dwindling and this time there

would be no good health to refloat them. Some income was still coming in from the group water contracts, retention money that had been held until the work proved satisfactory, but soon all this would finish. I applied for social welfare assistance but, as is the case today, there was nothing for a self-employed person.

As much as I hated the idea, I applied for disability allowance. An officer from the Department of Social Welfare came to visit me. She told me that disability allowance was means tested and that I would not qualify for it because I had too much land. I asked her what she suggested I do with the land. I couldn't give it to any of the children because they were not old enough to take it over and I would not sell it out on them. At that moment the children arrived home from school and threw their bags all over the kitchen. The official looked at them and I asked her how she thought I could feed the children as they couldn't eat land. She folded up her papers and said, 'I'll see what I can do and I'll be back to you in a week. I will have to discuss this with my superior.' She was true to her word. I was granted a reduced disability pension, something I loathed, but at the same time I was glad to eat humble pie.

Cloone had a committee that collected funds every year to send disabled or sick people from the parish to Lourdes with the diocesan pilgrimage. Peter Charles approached me and asked if I would be interested in going and I was grateful for his concern. I had tried other remedies, such as home cures, quacks, a seventh son, acupuncture and bio-energy, but nothing seemed to give me any relief, so I thought I'd try Lourdes. In June 1980 I was a member of the Ardagh and Clonmacnoise annual diocesan pilgrimage. A woman from Cloone, Minnie Dillon (RIP), was with me. There were about a hundred people in all on that pilgrimage, including helpers, a nurse, a doctor and the bishop, Cathal Daly. I found myself relaxing and enjoyed mixing with the other pilgrims, especially Minnie Dillon. She was a great character and we had some good laughs.

Our accommodation in Lourdes was in a hospital wing within the holy ground, close to the grotto. I was fairly independent and could do quite a bit for myself. I was getting accustomed to using my left hand and was much better at it than I had been at the start of this disease. While most of the disabled people on that pilgrimage rested between items on the schedule, I stole away on my own and visited the grotto unnoticed. I found this unscheduled visiting very rewarding. Even though there were hundreds of people there, probably thousands, I felt alone and could meditate. I stared straight at the face of the statue of Our Blessed Lady until I almost thought it moved. I made promises and bargains with her: I would be a good advocate and bring her message to the world if only she would cure me and let me back to my JCB.

At the end of the pilgrimage, a director from the complex gave our group a lecture about some of the cures and miracles that had occurred in Lourdes. There were not many but the director pointed out that any cure would have to go through a very rigorous medical board test before it was declared a miracle and that this could take years. But he did say that everyone who comes to Lourdes received some gift. He said, 'It may happen while you are here in Lourdes. It may happen when you go home, or it may happen in years to come. Eventually everyone will receive something.'

I returned home to my wife and family in Cloone, feeling really good. I believed that something positive would happen to me soon and living my life with one arm might not be too bad. I had prayed as I never prayed before, I had made a good Confession and Holy Communion. I was at peace with myself.

Then one day about six months later I found that the disease had spread to my left arm and hand. I became bitter and frustrated, furious with God, with Lourdes and the whole idea of religion. 'Why me?' I shouted. I had kept my end of the bargain and received nothing. Everything my hand touched fell to the ground. I had to use a straw to take liquids, and solid foods were fed to me as if I were a baby. I thought of Audie Murphy, who was awarded his country's highest decoration, the US Congressional Medal of Honor, for his part in the Second World War. In 1955, he took part in a cinemascope film that was based on his life's experiences, called *To Hell and Back*. I was going through hell with this disease but I knew there was no way back. I now had to watch my children doing the chores on the farm while I directed them in this work. Some of my younger children had never seen me as able-bodied. Physical work was a thing of the past for me. 'Boast no more your mighty deeds,' as James Shirley wrote in 'Death the Leveller'. Gone was the strong man of the 1950s and 1960s, replaced by a shrinking muscle-starved specimen.

I was still driving the car, although awkwardly. One day on my way home from Mohill with my wife and some of the children, I was coming up a hilly road near our house. A man I knew came around the corner on a scooter. He had a mental health problem and when he saw my car and its passengers, he panicked and almost lost control of his machine. I was faced with an imminent crash but my instincts directed me towards the ditch and the frightened man on his scooter got by with inches to spare. He was so scared he didn't even stop. Nobody was hurt, thank God, and I got the car out of the ditch, with the help of neighbours. The children even seemed to enjoy the near disaster. But I threw the keys on the kitchen table and said to Bridgie, 'That's the last time I'll drive a car.'

Bridgie and the children protested that it wasn't my fault, that I had done well not to kill that man. I knew this was true but I also knew that I should no longer be driving with my condition and that if I did have a crash it would be my fault. So I decided to quit while I was in the clear. I knew it was the right time to go, not when someone had to tell me. Bridgie took driving lessons and soon passed her test. I had achieved everything in the art of driving and I never regretted walking away from it with an unblemished driving licence.

21

Motor Neurone Disease

MND affects 400,000 people worldwide. In Ireland, approximately three hundred people have been diagnosed with MND and registered with IMNDA. The number of people with the disease does not change much: those who are diagnosed every year more or less replace those who die. In 1985 the Irish Motor Neurone Disease Association (IMNDA) was launched, the first organisation to recognise and support people who suffered from the disease in Ireland. The inaugural meeting was held on 1 May in the Friends' (Quaker) Meeting House, in Churchtown, Dublin. About sixty-five people attended and Carmel Ross was the founding chairperson. The first big fundraiser, the première of the Irish film *Eat the Peach*, was held in the Savoy Cinema, Dublin, in mid-March 1986.

One of IMNDA's founder members, Mary Callinan RIP, approached me that year and invited me to become a member. Even though I had had this debilitating disease for eight years, I didn't want to hear about the association. I hated the word 'MND'. I was completely in denial. Mary invited me to the association's AGM in the Westbury Hotel, Dublin and, reluctantly, I went. There I was introduced to many people with the disease, some who were far worse affected than I was. My eyes were opened and for the first time I realised that I was not alone, that others were suffering like myself. I immediately felt an emotional bond with these other patients.

Professor Michael Hutchinson had become a patron of the association and at that first AGM he expressed his optimism that there would be a cure for the disease. I found myself looking forward to the association's meetings and making friends with patients and committee members. Most committee personnel had lost a family member, a loved one or a friend to MND. I have attended most of the AGMs of the association since 1986, although some were very depressing, with professional people telling you and your family how to prepare for the inevitable – death. I sub-consciously built up a resistance to these lectures and just did not listen. One thing that greatly saddened me was when I made friends with people who were affected by the disease just like me and looked forward to another conversation with them at the following year's AGM but, alas, they were absent. Some were too disabled to travel; others had passed on.

One of the most disturbing aspects of this disease is lack of awareness and understanding among the general public and even among some of our healthcare professionals. It's hard for people suffering from MND to have to await the diagnosis of a celebrity, politician or someone with a high profile to increase awareness of the illness. I give high praise to Joan Brosnan Walsh, actress with

Andy with broadcaster Jimmy Magee at the AGM of the IMNDA in the Radisson Blu Hotel, Dublin, 2010.

Fair City; Paul Magee, sports commentator and ex-footballer, son of broadcaster, Jimmy Magee, and Michael Fitzpatrick, Fianna Fáil TD for Kildare. They all went public and greatly raised awareness of MND. God rest them all.

Joan Brosnan spoke on the *Late Late Show* about her illness and received a standing ovation as she explained her slurred speech and described her prognosis. Colm Murray, the well known sports commentator, more recently appeared on the *Late Late Show* and did a wonderful interview with Sean O'Rourke on RTÉ radio. He also participated in a documentary called *The Inside Track,* which had an audience of more than half a million viewers. He bravely volunteered to take part in tests of a new drug, organised by Professor Orla Hardiman, that may be beneficial to those who are diagnosed with MND in the future. Colm raised awareness of the disease more than anyone I've known, bringing the condition into every home in Ireland.

The key services IMNDA offers include home visiting by a specialist nurse, financial assistance towards home care help and the provision of specialist medical equipment and appliances on loan, free of charge, to their clients. The association also supports research into the causes and treatment of the disease through specific financial bursaries. Each year the association provides people with MND and their carers with a two-day weekend break in some popular hotel. The location is different each year and the weekend is a wonderful opportunity for patients and carers to mingle and exchange their life stories. It's by no means a doom and gloom meeting – far from it – and there's music, dancing, singing and other entertainment. I have been going to these weekend breaks for the past twenty years. Through them I have formed many new friendships and lifelong bonds. Each time I see the smiling face of a survivor of the disease it lifts my heart to know that they, like myself, are 'hanging in there'. This in itself is an indication that everyone does not die within the prognostic time.

The association's AGM takes place during this weekend, enabling patients and families to be brought up to date with the affairs of the association. We are very fortunate that a person of the calibre of Orla Hardiman, neurologist and internationally recognised expert, is researching a cause or cure for this terminal illness. Our medical patron is Professor Niall Tubridy, also a consultant neurologist. The sports broadcaster, Jimmy Magee, recently became a patron.

IMNDA's wonderful staff runs the office five days a week and there is a Freephone telephone line for patients. The staff do their utmost to help out in any way with equipment, care or counselling, or just listen to patients' tale of woe. I have been a beneficiary of their services, as the association provided me with computer technology that has given me back the ability to write and express myself.

Two years ago I was a member of a group of patients who were invited to meet the president, Mary McAleese, in Áras an Uachtaráin. We were wined and dined and it was an uplifting recognition of our plight. Being a member of this association has been a great help to me down the years.

On my 2008 pilgrimage to Lourdes, I met three wonderful

Andy with President Mary McAleese in Áras an Uachtaráin, April 2010.

people who had been diagnosed with MND. As well as the religious aspects of the pilgrimage, we shared plenty of laughs and humour. During my long survival with this disease, I haven't met any two people affected in the same way. For some it's their legs and for others it's their arms. Other people's speech, swallow and breathing are affected.

There is no day that goes by that I don't give thanks to God for the blessings I have enjoyed since I became involved with organisations like IMNDA. I get back tenfold what I put into them. I am a member of the British MND Association and I am also a member of ALS/MND in the United States. Every year five thousand people are diagnosed with MND in the United States. I keep in touch with these people through their newsletter and web page and through emails. Thanks to modern technology, the world has got a lot smaller. I tell my story with humour, laughter and hope. Given the opportunity, I try my utmost to lift the spirit of some distraught patient who is finding it hard to come to terms with their diagnosis.

I would like to emphasise that I am in no way complacent about my survival with this disease; nor do I indulge in the 'I'm all right' kind of thinking. I just take one day at a time and do the best I can.

22

Onwards and Upwards

It's surprising how a family can grow up almost unnoticed. My eldest son, Andrew, took over the running of the farm. My other son, Raymond, got married in London, in the same church as his parents, St Agnes's, Cricklewood Lane, without knowing anything about our marriage. Raymond and his wife Bernie had a daughter, Sharon, our first grandchild, a beautiful child.

Andrew married Mary Colum, from Drumlish, County Longford, and their first child, a boy, was born on 27 July 1988. A beautiful baby, he was christened Shane. After some early medical checks, it was discovered that he had severe cerebral palsy. The prognosis was that he would never walk, talk, or see and that he would have a reduced life expectancy. It was a devastating announcement for his parents and all of us. Baby Shane would smile his beautiful smile on hearing familiar voices, something that was very uplifting for the family, as all his other movements were involuntary. He was treasured by his parents and the rest of us.

Shane suffered from respiratory complications and had to have medical equipment to keep his airways clear. In January 1999, he developed severe breathing problems and had to be hospitalised. Despite the best of care and medical attention, Shane went to his eternal reward on 23 January 1999. His parents, brothers – Andrew born in 1989, Niall in 1992 and Mark in 1993 – and the entire family were heartbroken. Shane was a special child. He never had the opportunity to play or attend school, like other children, but on the day of his funeral, all his brothers' classmates formed a guard of honor in their little blue uniforms, to pay tribute to one of their own who was less fortunate than they were. They were a sight to behold.

On 27 July that year, Mary and Andrew had a baby boy, who

was christened Colm. From day one, he was a beautiful, healthy and lovable child. He had features familiar to Shane's and I do believe that he was a special gift as he had the same birthday as Shane. The Lord works in wondrous ways. Colm is now a young adult of thirteen. He calls to see me every day and his last words on leaving are, 'Grandad, do you want anything else done?'

In the early 1990s two of my daughters were in their early twenties and two were still teenagers. Despite our health problems, life went on. Looking back, I think I lived part of this period as if under an anaesthetic. I was too embarrassed to go out so if I had a drink it was in the house.

After my first pilgrimage to Lourdes, I was admitted to our Lady of Lourdes Rehabilitation Centre in Dún Laoghaire to have splints made for my wrists. The wasting muscles meant that they could not support themselves in any way. For any disabled person experiencing self-pity or 'why me?', this rehab is the place to go. I had never seen so many severely disabled people. I would go so far as to say that young people should be brought to this hospital on a visit, to see the destruction that accidents have caused to the bodies of some of the young people who are patients there. Seeing some of their own age group might prompt them to go a little lighter on the accelerators of their cars.

I was given a room at one end of the hospital and I had to walk through a ward of twelve beds every day. There was very little chat coming from any of the patients and the ward itself had a sombre atmosphere. I glanced at some patients as I passed through and saw that most of them were lying on their backs, with their heads supported in a padded position that they could move neither left nor right. They all seemed to be suffering from spinal injuries and none of them was old.

One morning I was passing through as usual when I heard a voice say, 'Here comes light foot.' I stopped at the end of this man's bed and asked, 'Are you referring to me?' He gave a slight smile, as much as his tightly-wedged head allowed, and said, 'I hear your step coming every morning before you enter the ward. To be truthful, I envy you. I would give all in the world to be able to walk like that.

What the hell has you here anyway?' I told him about my disease and that I had very little power in my hands and arms. His reply was, 'That's nothing. Most of us in this ward will never walk again and the best we can hope for is a wheelchair.'

Now more of the patients began to talk and enquired of me where I came from. Then the slagging started, with 'How many all-Ireland medals does Leitrim have?' The conversation turned into laughter. I was well able to answer them and, if the banter got too severe, I was the only one who could walk away. I found myself standing at the end of each bed on my way through every morning and sometimes on my return. We exchange great jokes and had to suppress our laughter at times. Before I reached the ward I would hear a voice say, 'Here comes Leitrim.'

I began to be worried that something would happen to one of them, for example could someone strain himself laughing? If this happened I would definitely get the door. One morning, as I completed my visitation, I thought my worst fears were about to be realised. I was on my way out of the ward when a staff nurse beckoned me into the office. I got in first, saying. 'I'm sorry for disturbing those patients.' She smiled. 'That's not what I called you in here for, quite the contrary. Do you realise how much happiness you have brought to those patients? They laugh every day now and they plan the jokes they are going to have for you tomorrow. Please continue to talk to them. You have done more than we could ever have done for them. And by the way, why don't you write a book?' I laughed so much I nearly fell. Write a book with my hands? You were as well asking a penguin to write a book. This nurse continued, 'You definitely have a lot of material in your head, if you could only get it down on paper. I'll talk to the occupational therapist to see if we could get you to type.'

The next morning I had an appointment with the occupational therapist. I had a typewriter in front of me and she started to hook me up to it. There were wires going in all directions and straps to hold my hands up in a certain position. I was like the bionic man, except that this contraption was not working. After two days of trying, I abandoned the effort. I'm a person who won't sit for long at any task as I like to get up and go. I explained to the therapist that I would have to have someone at home to put all this equipment on me and to get out of it would be another problem. The helpful therapist agreed with me.

The IMNDA became aware of my dilemma and referred me to the Central Remedial Clinic in Dublin for assessment about how I might operate a computer. There I met Ger Craddock, a computer technician. Ger tried me with various equipment but in the end we opted for a two-way switch pedal, operated by my right foot. This allowed me to move the cursor on to the appropriate letter on the keyboard, which was represented at the bottom of the monitor. After two days in the clinic, I finally typed the four letters of my name. Again I was about to give up but the technician said this was good and that he would deliver a computer to my home the next week for me to carry on from there. True to his word, he delivered the computer, again got me to write my name and presented me with two manuals that would direct me and explain the meaning of the icons. He shook my hand goodbye, giving me his phone number in case I needed it. 'Remember, Andy,' he said, 'learning to operate a computer is like learning how to ride a bicycle. Once you get your leg up, you're there.'

I worked at this machine every day until, after three weeks, I was able to write a short note to IMNDA, thanking them for giving me back the ability to write again, something I thought I had lost for ever. There is no reverse gear with motor neurone disease; once you lose a movement, it's gone. But with this technology, I had beaten the disease. The rest is history. Four years later, my book, *They Laughed at This Man's Funeral,* was published, a tribute to determination and above all to assistive technology.

The writing of this book was a great incentive for me. It was an enormous challenge, as each letter or punctuation character demanded an individual movement of the toe and heel with a foot-operated device to put it on the screen. It was a very tedious and time-consuming task but it was great brain therapy and took my mind off my illness.

At AGMs of the IMNDA, I become friends with one of the

*Andy with Deasún
Breatnach at the AGM of
the IMNDA in the Hodson
Bay Hotel, Athlone, 1999.*

committee members, Deasún Breatnach, who had been a journalist
and sub-editor with the *Irish Independent*. He encouraged me to keep
writing and said that he would check the script and proofread it and
make it ready for publishing.

Deasún had no experience of computers; nor had he any intention of learning. So there was only one way I could communicate
with him: write about ten pages, print them out and post them up to
him. He corrected them and sent them back down to me. Then I had
to insert Deasún's corrections into the file on the computer. I had
only a primary education and my writing and spelling skills were very
limited and there was no spell check or dictionary on this old Apple
computer. I had a Collins dictionary and consulted this, turning the
pages with my mouth. I went through hell and when the book was
finished, you would think that it was Fido the dog who had got at the
dictionary. I had to bin it.

I learned a lot from that well-informed man, Deasún. He was the
only one on the IMNDA board who had no connection whatsoever
with the disease but his heart went out to sick, disabled and

marginalised people. He went to the hospice to visit the dying and brought me along with him on occasion. He taught me more than I could have learned from any university lecturer, gave me confidence, never chastised me and even praised my intellect. He met me at Connolly Station and took me in his car to the hotel where the AGM was taking place, fed me my lunch and helped with any other little tasks I needed. When the AGM was over, we retired to the bar and partook of a considerable amount of the black stuff. I can say with certainty that the jokes and laughter I shared with him contributed greatly to my survival with this debilitating disease.

Deasún did not want any thanks, saying, 'It's my pleasure.' He took me to his home in Dún Laoghaire to meet his wife, Lucy, another example of his hospitality. He was anchored to nature. As he approached his home, he would start talking to the neighbours' dogs. Most of them were confined to the gardens at the back of the houses but every dog in the locality knew him and would let out a welcoming yelp. Then he would start to whistle to the birds, imitating them like a mockingbird. As we entered his house the birds flew around us. There was a big ash tree at his gateway of which he was very proud and he would say, 'Nobody will be allowed to cut this tree down in my lifetime.'

Deasún was born in Dublin but he loved rural Ireland. He would tell me about his time in the army during the war, when soldiers were sent down the country to help the farmers save the crops. He had really enjoyed this period. On 4 October 2007, Deasún went to his eternal reward. Lucy predeceased him by a few days, a fitting tribute to a loving marriage. They had lived for each other and now they died for each other. God rest them both. Motor neurone sufferers lost a great advocate and I lost a great friend. Until we meet again, *slán, a chara.*

My survival instincts were improving at a ferocious rate and no longer was I afraid of this terminal disease. My arms and hands were useless but inside I was bursting with energy, probably because my ability to do physical work had been taken away from me. I had a healthy body without arms or hands. I started taking note of my remaining abilities and realised how many I had. The IMNDA told me about a pilgrimage to Croagh Patrick, Mayo's holy mountain. Family members of people suffering from MND planned to climb the mountain to raise awareness and much-needed funds for the association. They invited me to come along and mingle with other patients, who would be enjoying the summer afternoon in the car park. There would be a barbecue and refreshments while we awaited the return of the family members participating in the adventure.

Immediately, I saw an opportunity for my pent-up energy that was craving a challenge. I told the association that I would join them on the day and attempt to climb the mountain to raise some funds for them. They were reluctant for me to attempt the climb but I said that even if I went up only a few hundred yards, it would raise awareness of the disease. I approached the *Leitrim Observer* and the *Longford Leader* to tell them what I was planning to do and to let them know that if anyone wanted to sponsor me, the funds raised would go to the association. The local newspapers were very helpful and printed articles about my participation in the adventure. Sponsorship started to roll in; there was no turning back now. On Sunday, 13 July 1997, I boarded a bus in Longford for the journey to County Mayo. Association colleagues greeted me in the car park at the foot of the Reek, with a barbecue of sausages and burgers, My friend Deasún also took on the challenge and negotiated the Reek successfully. He kept a watchful eye on my performance in case anything happened to me.

At one o'clock we were ready to start the climb. The mountain looked huge in the distance. On occasions, a cloud would cover the summit. Committee members approached me. 'Don't go up the whole way, Andy,' they urged. Two young men whose mother had MND accompanied me. They promised they would take care of me but I had to warn them, 'Don't put a hand on me as this will only affect my balance. Just pick me up if I fall down.'

The first stage of the climb was not too bad. We rested and I looked up. The summit was a half-mile away and stretching before me was a long trail of people clinging to the side of the mountain, like flies on a wall. My God, I thought, what's keeping them from falling off? My heart sank to my shoes. 'I'll never make it,' I said to myself. Then we started climbing again. I searched for the hero inside me and he responded. I plodded on in the footsteps of my young, energetic carers. After that I didn't look up, just kept repeating to myself, 'You can do it, Andy; you can do it.'

A group of four or five people were standing over a young man who had collapsed. Apparently his nerve had gone and he could not get up or move for his comrades. His companions waved us on, telling us that they were waiting for the Knights of Malta rescue team to arrive and take this man down by stretcher. This was a frequent occurrence for the team. Our group continued. When we rested again I leaned against a projecting shelf of heather. As I moved, the mound that I was leaning against for support, consisting of heather, stones and bog mud, collapsed and went rolling down the mountain.

Some time later I heard a shout, 'We're nearly there!' I lifted my head and there it was: a small, flat piece of rough, stony ground, with a little church to one side. There were no triumphant celebrations; that's the thing about climbing Croagh Patrick: you have achieved nothing until you get down in one piece. My thoughts now were for the people we had met coming down the mountain as we struggled up, some of them sliding on their behinds, their balance totally gone. I went into the little church, thanked God for giving me the stamina to complete this expedition and prayed for the people who had supported and encouraged me.

As I sat there, a thought came into my mind: how did they get the material to build a church on the top of this mountain? There were definitely no helicopters to transport the material and nobody could carry anything up the way we had come. I asked a steward and he told me that the other side of the mountain was not as steep. It was a longer way but a lot easier to negotiate and donkeys had brought the material up. He also told me that the real benefit of this pilgrimage was that it had to be done the hard way. We began the descent, my two eager carers out in front of me, exclaiming, 'We'll catch you, Andy, if you take flight!' I didn't slip once, even though carrying a stick or any other balancing equipment was physically impossible for me.

As we entered the car park, we were greeted by spontaneous applause from about a hundred of our companions who had been awaiting our return. In the hotel in Westport I drank a glass of beer and nothing I ever drank tasted as good as it. Tears of joy trickled down my cheeks. The adrenaline was pumping and winning the Lotto would have been an anti-climax in comparison with this exhilaration. The funds raised by this expedition were of great benefit to our association but the satisfaction I got could never be measured in money.

The following year, I again completed the climb and I can say with certainty that it was much easier. This time I concentrated on the challenge weeks before I took it on. I did not talk on the way up and I took some bananas with me, a great energy boost. I said good-bye to the mountain on this visit, as I would not be climbing it again. There's a time to reap and a time to sow, there is a time to hold on and there's a time to let go. It's very important to know when to stop. The IMNDA itself abandoned this fundraising activity because they thought some of their members might fall and get hurt and they had no insurance for this sort of eventuality.

I met a young man, John Kelly, from Tuam, County Galway, who had been diagnosed with MND. A bit like myself, he was a JCB driver, and the disease slightly affected one of his arms. We become great friends and he helped me in every way he could on the two trips to Croagh Patrick. His wife, Teresa, and his children came with him. They were involved with the Galway football team and he introduced me to some of the team in the hotel in Westport. In November 1998, Teresa and John came to Dublin to be at the launch of my book in Eason's, O'Connell Street, performed by the late Mick Lally, star of *Glenroe*. In earlier years, Mick had been a schoolteacher in Galway and, as it happened, John Kelly was one of his pupils. It was lovely to see the reunited teacher and pupil embracing.

John went into Beaumont Hospital to have further tests done by Professor Orla Hardiman. After some time she discovered that he had multi-focal motor neuropathy with conduction block, a very rare condition. It is not a terminal disease and is less destructive and more treatable than MND. The next time I met John he came running to me, saying, 'I haven't got MND. I'm over the moon. It's the best news I ever got. You told me all along that I didn't have MND, because my symptoms were a lot different from yours.' We both celebrated with the black stuff.

Some time later John was at a football game in Croke Park supporting his native county, Galway. Near the end of the game, he collapsed and, although he received attention from Dr Mick Loftus, it was not possible to revive him. He was rushed to the nearby Mater Hospital, where he was pronounced dead. May the Lord have mercy on his soul.

23

CASA and the Irish Wheelchair Association

On a fine day in May 1990, two women visited our home. They introduced themselves as Sister Mary Fox and Phil Murray, members of the Longford branch of an organisation called CASA (Caring and Sharing Association). CASA was founded by a group of volunteers in 1981. Its central purpose was developing friendships through social events for its members: sick, disabled and marginalised people. Now the organisation has branches in Dublin, Cork, Bray, Longford, Maynooth and Galway. The Longford group is extremely active, drawing people from neighbouring counties as well as the greater Longford area. I have been a member of this branch since 1990. No words could express the benefits I have got from being a member of this association.

On this first occasion, the women enquired about my disease and how I was coping. Mary Fox invited me to go to Lourdes with their association in June that year. I hesitated. To be honest, I had to control my rage in order not to insult the two do-gooders. I had been living with this terminal disease for thirteen years, afraid to move out, avoiding words such as 'progressive', 'incurable', 'invalid' and 'muscle-wasting', hibernating under the umbrella of my family. Also, as I eventually said to Mary Fox, 'I was in Lourdes ten years ago and got nothing.'

'You got nothing?' she replied. 'You have had motor neurone disease for ten years and more and you are doing fine, yet you say you got nothing. Not many people live for ten years with your disease.' The two visitors were staring at me. I was silent, probably hiding from the world, although not from God. An inner voice said, 'Go for it, Andy.' I knew then that I had to move out of this self-imprisonment. I couldn't just wait for mortality, as it seemed to be a long time in coming. The visiting ladies assured me that they would allocate me a good male carer, as it would be my first time not having the loving care of my family. Although it was difficult to imagine a complete stranger looking after me, I knew I would have to accept this in order to survive.

For the start of the pilgrimage Bridgie drove me to Longford, where I was introduced to other disabled people and their carers. My own carer would join me in Cork airport that afternoon. I was apprehensive but tried to relax as much as possible. The Longford people travelling on the pilgrimage were very supportive and attended to my every need; some of the people I met in Longford that morning are still among my best friends. I didn't have to worry about anything when we arrived at Dublin Airport as everything was arranged for me: luggage, passport, tickets and boarding pass. If I had any self-pity it soon disappeared when I saw, in Cork airport, many people far worse off than me.

In the airport I met my carer, an energetic man about twenty years my junior, also named Andrew. We got on very well. Andrew gave me my meal on the flight, another challenge for me. We arrived at our destination, the Mediterranean Hotel, at about midnight, had some refreshments and went to our room. All the accommodation there was suitable for disabled people. Andrew had me ready for bed in minutes. Next morning we were out of bed at eight o'clock. Andrew shaved and showered me and we were ready for breakfast in fifteen minutes. I asked him why he was so good at all this and his reply was that he and his wife had three small children, which gave him plenty of practice. Every year he spent one week of his holidays as a carer on the pilgrimage to Lourdes

When I thanked him for the way he had helped me that morning and complimented him on how good he was, he started to laugh. 'I'm not doing this for you,' he said, 'I'm doing it for myself. You'll never realise the amount of satisfaction I get from looking after a disabled person in Lourdes for five days. I have nothing to do for you, in comparison with some of the disabled people I've met.' When you register as a carer with CASA, you take whichever patient is allocated to you, so it could be a highly dependent person, not able to move, with every bodily function to be attended to and who would have to be wheeled to each scheduled event every day.

I found myself enjoying Andrew's attention and relaxed totally. When he asked if I would mind if he pushed a wheelchair to help someone else, I was delighted, as it gave me time to mix with the walking wounded. I attended all the religious functions but I did not get involved much in meditation or prayer; I just went with the flow. One night near the end of this pilgrimage, our group visited the grotto at midnight. We moved slowly around the cave in silent prayer. My carer rubbed my useless hands to the glazed rock and prayed, rubbing water that was oozing from the rock to my hands and forehead. The serenity of this holy place was awesome, with hundreds of people walking around in complete silence as if in a trance.

My carer took me to the water taps and washed my face with holy water. He realised that our group was on their way back to the hotel and whispered to me that we would have to get a move on, as he had to help push a wheelchair up that hill. He took off at a pace not

The Longford branch of CASA at Lourdes Airport, 2010.

recommended for the fainthearted but I matched him every step of the way. When we reached the main road, our group had crossed and the traffic was moving, leaving us standing on the kerb. I was glad of this because it gave me time to draw my breath. My carer had his hand up to his mouth and I knew he was laughing. I asked why. He became serious and said, in his beautiful Cork accent, 'You're the fittest invalid in Lourdes.' The traffic stopped and soon we were chasing our group again. That night I lay in bed for some time contemplating his comment, 'You're the fittest invalid in Lourdes.' To be truthful, I did not like it, although in another way. I knew that this man was paying me a compliment. Nobody had ever told me I was an invalid and I was still in denial as I felt that to be called an invalid was to be stigmatised.

The next day was our last in Lourdes. Our whole group visited the grotto for the last time. Thousands were queuing up and we had to wait, so some people knelt down in silent prayer. Ironically, I found myself kneeling in the very same spot where I had knelt ten years previously, in 1980. I looked up at the statue of our Lady, the very same statue I had begged for a cure ten years before. I felt remorse and embarrassment. How could I have been so naïve, so demanding, wallowing in self-pity and 'why me?' I had received the greatest gift bestowed on anyone and I had gone through hell because I had failed to recognise this gift. It took only a few words – 'You're the fittest invalid in Lourdes' – from a man I had known for no more than five days to rock me to my foundations.

I returned home from that pilgrimage with no physical improvement but I had a burning desire to get out, get involved and shake off the mantle of disability. When I saw the disabled people in Lourdes I realised that I was blind to the abilities I still had. I wanted to live to see my children and grandchildren growing up. After that trip to Lourdes I found great spiritual strength to accept the disease and learn what I could from the experience. This serenity gave me a power greater than myself. In fact, I took on challenges beyond my wildest dreams. I have been going on pilgrimages to Lourdes with CASA for seventeen years now. This pilgrimage is very important to people with disabilities and terminal illness.

In 1992 CASA invited me to join them for a five-day holiday break in the School for the Deaf in Cabra, Dublin. The pupils were on their summer holidays and the premises made available to our organisation. Voluntary carers were on hand to give us any assistance needed. They were superb and attended to everyone's needs effectively, with love and humour. About thirty disabled people and their carers took part. It was a wonderful holiday and a great get-together for us disabled people, with entertainments and visits to historic places prearranged by the association. We visited a folk park, 'Glenroe' farm in Kilcoole, Powerscourt Gardens and the newly-built shopping centre in Tallaght. We had meals in some of the top hotels in Dublin and Kildare. We even visited a farm and were made welcome by the owner.

As well as being immensely enjoyable, the week was a great learning experience for me as I mixed with other disabled people. One person in particular who caught my attention was Paul Walsh. He had been born without hands so it was no wonder I became interested in the way he was managing. I tried to learn as much as possible from the way he was coping, without staring at him or asking questions, as I knew that before long my hands and arms would be useless. One afternoon our group attended Mass and I took particular note of how Paul was reading his Mass leaflet. He held the leaflet between his toes, with one leg resting on the other, quite close to his face. It struck me how comfortable he looked, with no need for a desk or podium. But this information was useless to me, as I would strangle myself trying to get one foot across my knee. Paul had been disabled from birth and he had learned from a very early age to make maximum use of every available limb. Later on in that holiday break, I discovered that Paul needed no one to feed him. He held the eating utensil in his toe and with a lovely clean foot was able to sit at the table with the rest of us and eat his meals gracefully.

I became well acquainted with Paul on that holiday but I learned nothing from him that would help me with my physical disability. He had overcome his disability because he had it from birth and he knew no other way. I would never be able to do the things Paul was able to do but I learned a lot from his relaxed temperament and his inner strength in dealing with the cross that had come to him.

When we said our goodbyes after that holiday of 1992 the final greeting between Paul and me should have been recorded. I reached out my dangling hand to make contact with him; he smiled, caught my hand with his toe and shook it. Minutes later we were going our different ways but we both knew that we had given each other a great deal by our acceptance of our condition and by being at ease with the people around us. I have met Paul in Lourdes on many occasions since that holiday. He is a member of the CASA choir and writes his own music. We exchange emails and humour on occasion. Once I sent him an email that finished off: 'Best regards, handless Andy.' His return email ended: 'Go well, my friend, "toes" Paul.'

I will never forget the volunteers who helped us during that memorable holiday in Dublin but one in particular caught my attention. She was a beautiful girl of about twenty-two, who always appeared to be in good humour, laughing and smiling and making it her business to have contact with each disabled person. She would reach out with a hand on a shoulder, a hug, a smile or a joke, and the more a person was disabled, whether mentally or physically, the more she gave of herself. One day I asked her why she was always in such good humour. She said she had just qualified as a nurse and was over the moon as she had worked hard to get the qualification. She had not yet found a job but wasn't worried about that. She loved working with the CASA group but after that week, she said, 'It's over. I'm going to buy myself a car and have a good time for a little while.' I congratulated her and wished her the best of luck.

Before the week ended, she came back to me and said, 'Andy, I'm not going to buy that car and I'm not going to dwell on having a good time, just yet. I've volunteered to go to Somalia with Concern, as hundreds of children are dying of starvation there every day.' We went our separate ways after the holiday; Valerie was emotional as she hugged each one of us and asked us to pray for her.

On the evening of 23 February 1993, I was watching the six o'clock news when the newsreader said that an Irish nurse working with Concern in Somalia had been shot dead by gunmen. The newsreader named Valerie Place, aged twenty-three. A chill went down my spine as I saw the picture of the beautiful young woman accompanying the news story. It was the same Valerie we had said goodbye to a few months previously. I told my wife something about the kind of person Valerie was. She had been shot through the heart. I didn't wonder at this because Valerie had a big heart; as a matter of fact, she was all heart. Wendy Murphy, an Irish nurse who was with her on that tragic journey, said that Valerie had thrown herself to the floor of the car when the shooting started. But further shots were fired on the car as the aid workers tried to escape and Valerie was killed. May she rest in peace.

Valerie with a Somalian child.

Fr Aengus Finucane, who was travelling in a car in the same convoy as Valerie the day she died, paid tribute to her in the homily at her funeral: 'The short life of Valerie Place had its influence for good here in Ireland, in her home town and far beyond it. Her life had an influence on those who were her colleagues and on the children on whom, as a Concern volunteer, she lavished her love in Somalia. We are not here to renew our sadness but to thank God for giving us Valerie, a person we can remember with joy.'

I have now been a member of CASA for twenty-two years. The wonderful group of people behind the Longford branch never fails to involve me in its activities. I've made many friends in this organisation, especially with members of the Cork branch, and I was among CASA members who met the president, Mary McAleese in Áras an Uachtaráin.

To help fund its activities CASA has eight charity shops, as well as a bookshop above their restaurant, Ten Fourteen, in Clontarf. All income generated in this way goes to fund the charity's activities. They also have two break houses, one in Malahide and one in Swords, to offer respite care to disabled people. CASA's Christmas celebrations are held in the Burlington Hotel in early December. About four hundred people gather for these occasions, including disabled people, carers and family members, and I have been present at many of them. The programme begins with Mass, then there is a wonderful meal and dance, music and song, provided by some the country's top musicians, including Paddy Cole, Twink and Frances Black. On one occasion Taoiseach Bertie Ahern was present. The atmosphere at these Christmas celebrations is always electric, with disabled people shouting their heads off with laughter and song.

In October 2008, I went once again to Lourdes with CASA, a great opportunity, as Lourdes was celebrating the one hundred and fiftieth anniversary of the apparition of Our Blessed Lady to Bernadette. Tens of thousands of people of all nationalities and colour visited Lourdes every month during 2008. IMNDA liaises with CASA to have some of its patients included in the CASA pilgrimage.

I have not received any physical cure for my disease. It continues to progress but at a slower pace. I honestly believe that I have received the greatest gift that could ever be bestowed: that of acceptance and happiness. A terminal disease will take our bodies and our lives but it can never take our souls, our spirits or the people we are. Life itself is terminal. I will live for the moment.

I am no longer dying from this disease. I am living with it. When I am in Lourdes I don't pray for a cure; I pray that this acceptance will continue. 'Our Lady of Lourdes, give me the serenity to accept the things I cannot change.'

In 1995, I joined the Leitrim branch of IWA (Irish Wheelchair Association) in Carrick-on-Shannon, at the invitation of Pee McHugh, a man from my locality who had had a farm accident. His wife, Breda, volunteered to transport us to and from the meetings. This branch of IWA was in its infancy and in the process of renovating a section of the old vocational school in the town to provide a meeting room, office, kitchen quarters and a disability toilet. FÁS came on board to help us to convert the premises and

IWA head office contributed some funds. Sandra O'Loughlin was the driving force behind forming this branch.

Some of the meetings were disturbing, with a lot of arguments and raised voices. I felt I could well do without this hassle and one night I said I was leaving but Breda McHugh pleaded with me to stay on. Sandra struggled to keep meetings under control and made this branch of IWA into a successful organisation, providing transport and assistance to disabled people and wheelchair users in Leitrim, Roscommon and further afield.

Pee McHugh lives about three miles from me and is a year younger than me. We didn't have the opportunity to get to know each other in our young lives, probably because I spent twelve of my early years in England. We had things in common, though: both of us were married with six children and anchored to farm work and the land.

Pee, a progressive farmer, was disposing of slurry on his out farm on 23 March 1990. He had delivered one load of slurry and his second load had filled. Pee moved up to the front of the tanker to raise the control lever but as it turned out he didn't get to raise it: this is the last memory he has of that evening. Luckily for Pee, a man by the name of Mickey Flanagan came to deliver a ton of meal from McCarren Brothers Mills. It was Mickey's first time at the out farm. He heard the tractor engine running at high rpm and approached to find out where the meal was to go. To his horror, he discovered Pee lying lifeless in a pool of slurry. He alerted some neighbours, who called for a doctor and ambulance. Before long, Dr Dolan arrived and administered whatever medical help he could. They placed Pee, slurry and all, on the back seat of Dr Dolan's car and they sped off and met the ambulance coming with all sirens roaring. He was transferred to the ambulance and put on a drip and taken to Sligo hospital.

Pee regained consciousness after six weeks and saw nurses moving around the room. He thought he was having a nightmare and covered his head to go back to sleep. Eventually he realised that he wasn't in his own bed and got quite confused. He called to one of the ladies in white and asked where he was. She told him he was in Sligo hospital as a result of an accident on the farm and when he asked her how he was, she replied, 'Pee, thank God you are alive but you lost your arm.'

Some time later what she said registered in Pee's brain but he thought to himself that it couldn't be true. He was lying there without ache or pain and he thought there was only one way to find out. He threw off the bedclothes and went to raise his two hands but only his right hand came up. Pee told me he cried bitterly that evening when he thought of his wife and their six little children back at home.

Breda arrived every evening to visit him. With her reassurance – she was a nurse and had studied psychology – Pee was eventually able to accept his predicament and was thankful to be alive. He was transferred to the rehab in Dún Laoghaire after six months in Sligo. He eventually came home for good on 16 March 1991, fifty-one weeks after his accident.

Because of an event before his accident and another while he was in rehab, Pee is convinced that it was a black-out that caused his problem. He had got a knock on the side of his head six years previously and while there was no outward sign of damage, there was some internal bleeding capable of causing a blackout. This could also be a contributory factor to calcium building up in Pee's left knee and ankle, which has left his knee in a fixed position and his walking ability minimal. He can manage to walk a little on floored surfaces with the aid of a tripod; he also uses a wheelchair and, on occasions, a golf buggy, which is a great asset as he can negotiate the fields to inspect his farm and cattle.

In 2001, Pee's wife, Breda, died. May she rest in peace. This was another severe blow for him and his family but he held his composure and focused on the future. That is why I admire this man, who is always in good humour and ready to help out anyone in difficulties. We have become good friends over the past seventeen years but it is our disability that has brought us closer together. We don't patronise one another with phrases or compliments. It's a matter of, 'Don't moan, just carry your cross.'

I have met many disabled people like Pee McHugh by joining

organisations such as CASA and the IWA. They have inspired me beyond belief and have made me look at my own disability as a minor interruption. These people are far too numerous to mention but meeting each of them was a signpost for me to carve out my own destiny and search for the power within. Sometimes when I mix with these people, I find myself asking, 'Who are the disabled?' If we could inject some of their initiative, enthusiasm, courage and determination into able-bodied people, we would have a different nation today.

During my time as a disabled person I have made friends all over the world and thoroughly enjoy my involvement with the organisations of which I am a member. I feel at one with the people involved, regardless of their status in life and the reason they are disabled. Many years ago, while I was a member of the Leitrim branch of the Irish Wheelchair Association, we were invited to a cross-border meeting with disabled people from Northern Ireland. At that time the Troubles were at their peak. It was a two-day conference and we stayed overnight in Kesh, some distance outside Enniskillen. The two groups mingled well together although one could sense some tension.

The Northern spokesperson welcomed us and spoke about the advantage of cross-border cooperation, as regards accessing funding from both sides of the border. It was our turn next to say something. I had been chosen to give this presentation with very little notice. I thanked the Enniskillen disabled group for their kind invitation. I explained that there are no boundaries, borders or divisions of religion, colour, creed, politics or ethnicity as far as disabled people are concerned: 'Together we are united, fighting for better conditions for disabled people. We are brothers and sisters who happened to be disabled and we will not let any outside force drive us apart.'

Any tensions dissolved straight away and there were tears in the eyes of members of both groups. We spent the next two days enjoying one another's company and we invited the Enniskillen disabled group to Mohill, where we had another great meeting and celebration.

24

The Leitrim Association of People with Disabilities

One day in 1996 a woman came to my home. She introduced herself as Sister Emanuel Farrelly, a native of my own original parish, Aughavas. She told me that she was a Sister of Mercy and had been a teacher in Marian College in Mohill and that she had taught one of my daughters. She was appointed principal of the college but then she was diagnosed with MS. She accepted her cross with great courage and worked on for as long as she could but finally had to give up working. Not an easy thing for anyone in their early forties, as I have experienced.

Sister Emmanuel asked me to call her Patsy, saying, 'I was born in 1950, just up the road from you.' We had attended the same national school, Corduff, we were both baptised and had made first Confession, first Holy Communion and Confirmation in Aughavas church, yet our paths had never crossed. I was seventeen years older than her and had probably been in England when she was growing up.

When she had to give up teaching Patsy did not walk away into the wilderness. She did not bury her head in the sand or wallow in self-pity or 'why me?' She had a dream to set up an organisation to represent sick and disabled people in Leitrim and further afield. On 8 May 1996, her dream became a reality when the Leitrim Association of People with Disabilities was launched. Patsy was chairperson, secretary, treasurer and manager. She and Marie McGuinness, another MS patient, who is still actively involved with the association, worked for months without pay or reward to get this organisation afloat.

Patsy approached FÁS and the North Western Health Board, as it was then, pleading with them for funding, so that she could employ some personal assistants (PAs) for disabled people, in order to return these people to independent living in their own homes. She applied to the National Rehabilitation Board for a grant towards start-up expenses, as well as to the People in Need trust fund. Both these applications were successful and Patsy sought local business sponsorship on a once-off basis. Many businesses in the area gave generously to the appeal. FÁS promptly responded to Patsy's request for a community employment scheme to provide PAs and sixteen people were employed.

Patsy explained the purpose of her visit: she wanted me to join the association. People with various disabilities had come on board but they had no one with motor neurone disease and she felt I would be a great asset to the organisation. I couldn't refuse this woman, as she seemed to me to have initiative, drive, education and enthusiasm that would really help disabled people. It didn't end there. Once she had roped me in, she took out some more papers from her briefcase, saying that she wanted me to become a director of the organisation. I pleaded with her that I was satisfied just to be a member but she was having none of it so I signed the appropriate papers with my stamper. She said it was important to have four or five directors before she submitted the final draft of the constitution of the Leitrim Association of People with Disabilities for affiliation with the Disability Federation of Ireland (DFI).

I started to attend the meetings and was totally overwhelmed by the disabled people I met. Their momentum and enthusiasm were evident. The association arranged an extra-mural certificate course entitled 'An Introduction to Community Development in Relation to Disabilities', for September 1967. In Drumshambo, twenty-five of our people took part in that course, including officers, carers, disabled people and some PAs.

The course was intended to raise awareness around disability issues and develop the participants' confidence and self-reliance. Kevin Kelly, a highly regarded lecturer, gave the course. If there were ever such a thing as a whiz kid talking, it was he. He jumped on the floor and wrote on the blackboard, explaining to us how to pursue our goals. He was speaking so quickly that I don't think any of our disabled group knew what he was on about. He told each one of us to set a goal for ourselves, write it down on a placard and to hang it in our house where we would see it often during the day. This way we would log it into the subconscious and we were not to give up trying until we had achieved our goal.

Kevin told us about his own goal. He was writing a book called *How When You Don't Know How* and he intended to make it a bestseller. At this point he was so worked up, chalk in hand and drawing on the blackboard, that his feet were barely touching the ground. When he stopped for a brief moment and asked if there were any questions, Patsy said, 'There's a man here who is writing a book with his foot.' Stunned, he asked, 'With his foot?' 'Yes,' said Patsy, 'he's here sitting beside me.' Kevin asked me about my arms and hands and my disease and how I was writing this book and I explained to him about the equipment I had for the computer and the foot mouse I was operating. He seemed sceptical about my explanation, so he asked me if I would bring in the script, which I did the following day. He was dumbfounded, not just by what I had written but by the simple fact that I could write anything with my useless hands and arms.

We all took on a project and set ourselves a goal under the watchful eye of this energetic lecturer. When the course was completed, the projects were submitted to the National University of Ireland. Six months later we were invited to NUI Maynooth. Each one of us received an extra-mural diploma, a certificate in community development and working with the disabled. We learned a lot from Kevin Kelly. We learned to believe in ourselves and gain self-confidence; we were ready to take on any task, knowing that we were all worthwhile, just because we were alive. To my delight I discovered that this genius of a lecturer also learned something. I found the following on his web page.

The article is called 'Take Ownership':

'Accepting Responsibility is the Key

'If where you are now is not exactly where you want to be, how do you move to a better place?

'Your first step is simply to accept responsibility for your life.

'In 1997, I was asked to speak to a group of people who suffered from a range of illnesses. The participants were the source of much inspiration to me, none more so than sixty-four-year-old Andy McGovern. Andy had been diagnosed with motor neurone disease in 1976. The life expectancy for sufferers of this central nervous system disease is between two and five years.

'For a self-employed father of six children aged between three and sixteen years of age, this was the worst possible disaster for Andy. Incredibly, twenty-one years after the diagnosis, Andy published a book, *They Laughed at This Man's Funeral.* He wrote it with his right foot. He climbed Croagh Patrick, the west of Ireland's pilgrimage mountain, twice. It is a very difficult challenge that many very fit and active people avoid. And today he surfs the worldwide web with his right foot.

'What happened in those two decades to enable Andy to live a remarkable and fulfilling existence? Two to five years, the experts said, not twenty-one.

'For him, the answer was simple. "I started to accept my lot, realizing that, in a strange sense, I was better off than many of the people I met in Lourdes and along the way. From then on, my focus changed from problems and obstacles to possibilities and magnificent challenges; to celebrating each moment as opposed to stewing in self-pity. I found that acceptance was the first step towards inner healing."

'I was inspired and moved by Andy's story and his advice. Listening to him, it was obvious to me that accepting and taking responsibility were indeed an important step in our development. I realised then that, in my own life, whenever there were challenges, I was the problem but I was also the solution.'

Everyone was determined to make the Leitrim Association of People with Disabilities a success. We elected a new committee, with Margaret Elomari as chairperson, and she did a tremendous job. On her retirement, I was elected chairperson. To be truthful I wasn't very happy in this position but I accepted all the unanimous

LAPD directors' meeting 2010. Back row from left: Tom Lavan, John Rooney, manager Rosaleen Kielty, Maureen McNabola, Peter McHugh, Brigid McGourty, Martina Fox, Andy McGovern; front row (from left): Izalda Carmody, Tom Murphy and Howard Cusack.

decisions made by the board. This was the role of the chairperson as far as I was concerned and I never had to use my casting vote. It was a turbulent time for our association, a period I'm not going to write much about. We were very cramped in a small office with just one small toilet and washbasin. All our meetings were held there, with four or five of our staff working on computers at the same time. It became evident that we would have to get new accommodation. The number of members, personal assistants and people on the board of management had grown to such an extent that the atmosphere at meetings become frustrated and irritable. I was greatly relieved when these meetings were over.

In February 2005, the association appointed a new manager, Rosaleen Kielty, who was a student on the extra-mural course we completed in 1997. From day one it became apparent that she was well in control of her job and a great calm was born. Staff members, committee members, board of management and personal assistants all worked in harmony once more. I would describe our new manager by adapting a line from Rudolph Kipling's poem, 'If': she could keep her head when all about her were losing theirs.

Rosaleen was adamant that the first aim of the association should be to get new office accommodation. The whole committee searched for a site or suitable premises in the town of Mohill and surrounding districts but these were the Celtic Tiger years and property prices were sky-high. One week I spotted premises near Mohill for sale in the *Leitrim Observer*. They were on good level ground with easy access. I told Rosaleen about them and she made arrangements with the auctioneer to visit. All the committee members were in agreement that we should purchase these premises, if the price was right. The price was high but finally we bought them for €190,000 and employed an engineer and an architect to convert them into offices that would be accessible for people with all sorts of disabilities.

When my term expired, Tom Murphy was elected chairperson. Tom was a wheelchair user, as a result of an accident in Luton in 1971. He became the driving force behind the project and not many days passed that he did not visit the site to instruct the builders on the subject of disability issues. Many people were instrumental in the success of this ability centre but Tom Murphy surpassed everyone in his determination to make the project a dream come true. The others are too numerous to mention individually but they all deserve great credit.

The premises themselves consisted of four offices, a reception area with a large desk, a meeting room, a state-of-the-art kitchen with everything accessible for disabled people and disability-friendly toilets and washbasin. The centre had under-floor heating that was fuelled by a wood chip boiler from outside and solar panels on the roof. But the jewel in the crown was surely the electronic lift, the first such lift for the people of Mohill. I was present the day it became operable and the first wheelchair user to try it out was none other than the gallant Tom Murphy. As he emerged from the lift on the top floor, he let out a bit of a yahoo. He proceeded at high speed to the big window overlooking the town. There were tears in his eyes as he turned around to me and said, 'Andy, that's the first time that I have viewed Mohill town from upstairs in thirty-eight years.' The cost of the finished ability centre was in excess of €600,000. The Celtic Tiger was roaring in our economy but he didn't get through Mohill without our disabled people plucking a few hairs from his backside.

On 9 May 2008 President Mary McAleese officially opened the new centre. It was a great occasion for our able-bodied and disabled people who had worked together to achieve this goal. Patsy/Sister Emmanuel, now honorary president of our association, came from the nursing home that day to celebrate with us. As the President cut the tape and declared the centre open, it was hard not to think about this woman's vision, as she launched what seemed like an impossible venture.

I gained wonderful experience and self-confidence by joining these associations for sick, disabled and marginalised people. The people I met never ceased to amaze me and there was one in every association who drew my attention and helped me in some way to be more at ease with my own problem. I took particular notice of Tom Murphy, a man confined to a wheelchair, paralysed from the waist down. At the early age of twenty-two, he was working in a heading in a small tunnel on the outskirts of Luton when the roof collapsed and he received severe spinal injuries. For a young married man with two small children, this was the worst possible scenario. It was twenty-six years later that I first met Tom and we talked about our different disabilities. He couldn't understand how I was managing without hands or arms and I couldn't understand how he was getting on without legs. So the best we could do was laugh at our inadequacies.

I soon discovered Tom Murphy's many hidden abilities. He could drive his car as well as any able-bodied person; indeed, far better than some. He transferred from his wheelchair to the driving seat with no problem whatsoever. He then dismantled the wheelchair, removed the easily adjustable wheels, placed them in the back seat of the car, then lifted the lightweight section and placed it on the back seat. He was now ready to take on any journey, maybe drive to Dublin Airport to pick up some relative on their way home from England or America. He could reassemble that wheelchair in seconds and negotiate his way through the complicated airport with speed and ease. Absolutely amazing. He said to me, 'Andy, once I get behind the steering wheel of the car, my disability vanishes.'

Tom was great company. On one occasion the Carrick-on-Shannon branch of the IWA invited us to a night out in Ballinamore. After a good meal in a hotel, we retired to Pat Joe Reynolds's lounge bar for a night of song, music and Irish dancing. Tom and I took up our position near the bar and we drank plenty. The place was packed to capacity. A group of English tourists were close to us and were fascinated by our banter and laughter. It was quite obvious that our condition (one in wheelchair and the other drinking through a straw) amazed them and they insisted on buying us several drinks. We were on a high when someone approached Tom and asked him to sing a song. Before he moved up to the microphone, he asked me, 'What will I sing? Will I sing a rebel song?' 'Of course,' said I, 'What else would you sing in Ballinamore?'

There were loud cheers and applause for Tom as he made his way up to the microphone but when he announced that he was going to sing 'James Connolly', the cheers become louder again. When he reached the line: 'God's curse on you, England, you cruel-hearted monster//Your deeds they would shame all the devils in hell', the cheers were so loud I thought the roof would cave in. Tom finished the song to sustained applause and made his way back to where I was sitting, wondering what our newfound friends from England thought of this performance. Well, I hadn't long to wait for an answer. They were all over right away, clapping Tom on the back, One said, 'My old dad came from County Donegal,' and another, 'My mum was from County Cork. You see, we are all Irish.' Again, the drinks started to pour in. Good man, Tom. What a night!

The association bought a new wheelchair bus to provide transport for our disabled people and in 2011 we secured a wheelchair boat so that our disabled members could enjoy boat trips on the beautiful lakes of Leitrim.

I love socialising and meeting people, whether it be at association meetings for the disabled or connecting with the able-bodied. I go to Mass most Sundays and of course I sample the beverage afterwards and meet up with some schoolfriends of long ago. I frequently visit McCaffrey's bar and grocery, close to Aughavas church. When I was growing up, the premises were known as Lee's; later the pub was called John Eddie Brady's. Although the business changed hands, the atmosphere, with its joking and banter, is the same as ever.

One particular Sunday in April 2005, I took up my position as usual at the right-hand side of the bar, known as the geriatric wing, although some who use it would not like the 'geriatric' tag. There was a capacity crowd that Sunday as there was a big football match in Croke Park. The hum of laughter and conversation is something I have always enjoyed being part of.

Most of the people in the bar were well known to each other, or at least someone belonging to them was known. But then two strangers came through the open door. They looked for a vacant position at the bar but there was none, so they walked up to where I was sitting. There was one vacant spot beside me where at least they could order a drink. I beckoned one of them to the space and he smiled and said, 'Thank you.' They ordered a glass of beer and a cup of tea. On hearing their accent, I started the conversation with, 'Ye are strangers to this part of the country.' One of the men replied, 'Yes, I'm from New York and my friend, Joe, is from Canada.' Joe said, 'My name is Joe Meehan and my ancestors came from Drumkeeran. They emigrated in the 1800s and this is the first time I've been to Ireland.' I said, 'You're very welcome back to the land of your ancestors.'

My new companions were very relaxed and seemed to be enjoying the atmosphere in the pub. I was drinking my usual glass of Guinness through a straw. Joe, the man drinking the tea, asked, 'I hope you don't mind me asking but did you have an accident?' 'No,' I said, 'but on the other side of it, you could say that I ran into God.' The two men laughed and I explained to them that I had a disease. 'Don't worry,' I said, 'it's not contagious.' Again, there was laughter. I said, 'I don't suppose that either of you have ever heard of motor neurone disease? It's a rare disease but that's what I have.'

There was silence and my two new acquaintances had sombre expressions. I did detect the sound of the cup vibrating against the saucer in the hand of Joe. 'My God,' said Joe, 'I've just been diagnosed with the disease. How long have you got it?'

I replied, 'Twenty-eight years.'

Joe said, 'My neurologist told me that I have only two years to live and all the information on websites relating to this disease indicates the same life expectancy. What are you taking for it?'

'Nothing.' I said, 'there is no tablet or a cure for this disease.' He knew himself that this was true. He seemed shocked and chose a stool to sit down. 'I have travelled four thousand miles from Canada to visit the birthplace of my ancestors, just to walk the land that my forefathers tilled for survival. And what has happened? I walk into a country pub in an isolated part of Leitrim and up to a man with the same disease. According to the experts, one person in 40,000 contracts this disease. Is this fate or what? Had there been another vacant spot anywhere in this bar, I would never have met you.'

Joe asked his friend to go out to the car and fetch a camera to have his picture taken with me. He wanted to buy me a drink but I told them that I had gone past my time in the bar as arrangements would have been made for my dinner. He fully understood. He could not get over the coincidence of his travelling from Canada and meeting another man with the same rare disease. And indeed I was amazed myself. We exchanged email addresses and websites and I told them where they would find suitable accommodation. The next morning I had a phone call from the lady who owns the guesthouse to thank me for sending the two lovely gentlemen to her premises. Joe emailed me on his return to Canada, delighted that he had reached his goal: to walk the lands of his ancestors before MND took away his ability to walk.

Joe and I kept in touch by email nearly every month. His condition deteriorated quickly, so that each email reported that the disease was affecting more of his muscles. First, he walked with a stick, then a walking aid, later a wheelchair and finally a motorised wheelchair. His family was very good to him, taking him on trips to different countries. His breathing and respiratory functions then became affected and he was admitted to a nursing home. His emails became less frequent and more upsetting to read. On 10 July 2006, one year and three months after that surprise meeting, I received the following email with the subject, 'A chance meeting of two men with MND'.

'10 July 2006

'Dear Andy

'Each day as I lie here I think of our meeting under the divine hand of God at the sacred and holy shrine of St McCaffrey's Bar. I can picture it still in my mind's eye and your success with this debilitating disease has always given me comfort, as your sense of humour gives me joy.

'My youngest daughter, Christine, is typing this letter for me, as my breathing is so weak now I am on a lot of drugs to keep me calm but they also keep me sleepy. They expect my end time on this side of Tír na nÓg to be any day now.

'So tell all the holy brothers who make their daily pilgrimage and gather daily at the sainted, venerable, and holy shrine of St McCaffrey's to keep a prayerful vigil as they raise their Guinness and say a prayer to remember my wife, Rena, and me.

'Andy, you have been like a brother to me and I've read and saved any email you have sent. This is my last email and I wanted to wish you well and assure you of my continued prayers.

'Your brother,

'Joe'

This arrived three days later.

'To all the friends and acquaintances of Joe Meehan

'Joe passed away on July 13 in North Battleford at Regional Care. His funeral will be held at St Joseph's Church on Tues July 18 2006 at 10:30am. There will be a celebration of Joe's life in the gymnasium at John Paul II Collegiate at 7:00 pm on Tues July 18.'

May he rest in peace.

25

Profiles in Courage

I undertook all sorts of challenging physical work in my able-bodied lifetime and mastered every chore and occupation I faced. I felt I owed this to my parents from a young age and then that I owed it to myself. I had to take on the world and prove that I could make it on my own. That's what growing up is all about. Later I had to secure a standard of living for my wife and six children and I embraced this task with great vigour and energy. I'm not looking for any praise, credit or recognition as it was my duty and responsibility. Nobody said that I was good, bad or indifferent at any of these responsibilities but what surprised me was that when I became disabled and 'useless' in my midlife, I started to receive awards and accolades for the way I was dealing with being useless.

In 2000, the local branch of IWA presented me with the Cúchulainn Award, a bronze statue, in recognition of my work with the association and my writing skills. I was bussed to Dublin, where a celebration dinner for disabled award-winners from all over Ireland took place in the restaurant in Croke Park. The then Taoiseach, Bertie Ahern, welcomed us all and spoke highly of our achievements. As I accepted this award I smiled and said to myself, 'I have witnessed tougher times than this.'

In 2003 I received an invitation from Leitrim County Council to attend an awards ceremony in the council offices but I could not attend as I was on my way to Lourdes that week. The council replied that it would postpone the awards ceremony until after I got back. The chairperson of the county council had recently established a new award, the Cathaoirleach (chairperson) Annual Award, to honour people whose work had contributed greatly to the image of County Leitrim. I was surprised to find that I was one of the seven nominees for 2003. All the nominees were given accolades for their great work and then the overall winner was announced. I was amazed and very humbled when my name was read out. I received a bog oak trophy, a cheque and a framed picture of the Leitrim County Council coat of arms, presented to me by the then chairperson, Jim Joe Short. I was unable to receive any of these with my useless hands and arms but my little grandson, Niall, was there to assist me and he had the full of his arms of trophies home with him. I smiled to myself, wondering why I never got any recognition like this for carrying the hod.

Twelve years ago, I was in my local pub, McCaffrey's in Aughavas, having a few glasses of Guinness through a straw. On this particular night a student teacher in Cloone national school approached me. She said her inspector had suggested that she get a disabled person to speak to the children she was teaching about disability issues so she asked me if I would oblige. I hesitated for a few moments, as public speaking is not something I like, and dealing with children can be very demanding for an unqualified person. Eventually I told this young teacher I would do it. Arthur Guinness gave me the courage to say yes.

The very next morning, a Monday, the phone rang. It was my student friend. She said, 'I'm sending Mammy up for you to come down and talk to those children today.' I was so taken aback that I didn't know what to say: the courage of Arthur Guinness had by then died within me. I felt like making an excuse but I knew that some day I would have to face up to my fear. So I said yes, send Mammy up. Worse again, I realised my two grandchildren were in her class. What would they think when their grandfather started to lecture about disability? Would they be embarrassed or would other children mock them? Anyway, the die was cast and there was no way back. At eleven o'clock the mother of this student teacher, also a teacher, came for me. I had rehearsed nothing and in my apprehension I could not think of anything to say but I whispered a wee prayer and my courage gradually returned

When I entered the classroom, there were at least thirty openmouthed, wide-eyed children staring at me, including my two grandchildren, who had no prior notice of my appearance. The teacher introduced me: 'This is Andy, who is going to talk to you about disability.' She sat me down at a table, then disappeared to the back of the classroom. I said in my best voice, with a big smile, 'Good morning, children. I am a disabled person and I've got absolutely no power in my hands or arms.' I stood up and showed them my useless hands and arms. They listened attentively and none of them even smiled. It was obvious that they wanted to hear more.

I explained to them that everyone experiences some disability in their lives. No one is exempt. There is nobody more disabled than newborn babies, who cannot walk, talk, stand, clean themselves or feed themselves. But the good thing about this disability is that from day one, babies are emerging from it and they don't remember it and therefore are in no way embarrassed by it. At the age of seven or eight, they have shaken off the mantle of this disability.

At that moment I felt I had captivated the children. I don't know where I got the inspiration from – it must have been that wee prayer – but I knew they were all interested and none of them had ever thought that at one time they had been disabled. I talked to them about different disabilities and said that the worst disabilities were the ones no one sees, such as fears and phobias. I mentioned a young lad in the parish who has some spinal injuries and walks with the aid of aluminium crutches. On occasion, he reads the lessons at Mass. He goes up to the altar, making a lot of noise with his equipment, and nobody can match his confidence or his ability at reading those lessons. He proceeds back down the church to his seat, again making plenty of noise, without a care in the world.

At the back of the very same church, there are five or six strapping, young, able-bodied men, standing with their backs to the wall. They choose this position rather than having to go up the church. They are probably making remarks and giggling about some woman's hat or other people's clothes but they do not have the courage to go up three or four seats in the church in case someone might look at them. I asked the children which people were disabled in that church. A flutter of hands went skywards and they all shouted, 'The men with their backs to the wall.'

'Yes,' I said, 'that's what I meant when I spoke to you about hidden disabilities such as phobias. If we could all have the confidence and composure of that young man who walks with crutches, how different the world would be.' I talked about other disabled people in the parish and how they dealt with their problems, reminding the children that a disability ignites initiative and can be the very thing that prompts a person to pursue another goal. I advised them to focus on a disabled person to help them appreciate all they had but usually took for granted.

The teacher said, 'It's break time. Say thanks to Andy.' The children all made a dash for me, clustering around me like chickens around the mother hen. They wanted to see my hands and some of them touched them to see if they were real. The teacher insisted on my having my picture taken with the children. I had a few pounds in my top pocket and I asked the teacher to go over the road to Doherty's shop and get each of the children a bar of some confectionery. She replied, 'You have given them enough,' but I insisted, saying, 'They have given me more than words can say.' The mother teacher left me home. I felt ten feet tall, as what was once a frightening challenge for me had become a great triumph. The bond I created with those smiling children is something that will live with me for ever and I didn't need to receive any trophy for this achievement. I had learned a lot from the presentation: I had overcome my fear of public speaking and realised that nerves were not my enemies but my friends, helping me to stay focused.

In 2007 people with different kinds of disabilities came together under the auspices of Leitrim Association of People with Disabilities (LAPWD) to tell their personal stories by creating a video, *Profiles in Courage*. The seven people chosen were Pee McHugh, Maureen McNabola, Tom Murphy, Joey Gallaher, John Rooney, Margaret Kelly and myself. The video was intended as an educational tool to heighten awareness of disability issues. The project received support from the National University of Ireland, Galway, the Programme for Peace and Reconciliation, the County Leitrim Partnership and Leitrim County Council.

The seven of us told our story of how we coped with our

disability and the film focused on our achievements and showed us going about our everyday chores. The video was sold to other groups for the disabled all over Ireland and it was suggested that we do a presentation in the secondary schools of County Leitrim. County Leitrim Partnership provided us with a course to prepare us as facilitators for the presentation of the video. It was decided that two of the people who had participated in making the video would take turns talking to students about what was in the film. This was a challenging undertaking and it took some negotiating to discipline some of the students. Sometimes we encouraged them to use a wheelchair or do something without hands or arms. We had some of them blindfolded to see how they managed with impaired sight. All these situations were replicas of the disabilities with which the seven participants were living every day.

My co-presenter in Manorhamilton Comprehensive School was Joey Gallaher, who was in a wheelchair. He had been a taxi driver in his able-bodied life but hit a bridge on his way home one night and was paralysed from the waist down as a result of this accident. He had accepted his fate and was getting on with his life, driving a beautiful, specially-adapted Mercedes with hand controls.

We showed the film to a large group of students and got a great reception. The teacher in charge asked the pupils, 'Have you any questions for Joey or Andy?', something that neither of us anticipated. A girl put her hand up and asked Joey, 'What would you like to do if you had your able-bodied life back again?' Joey hesitated for a few seconds, then said, 'If I was able-bodied again. I would love to climb Croagh Patrick.' Then it was my turn. She asked me the same question. I thought of Joey and his beautiful Mercedes and replied, 'I climbed Croagh Patrick twice in my disabled condition but I would love to be able to drive Joey's Mercedes.' There was an outburst of laughter from the class because each of us wanted what the other one had. The class applauded and two of the students came up and presented each of us with a little box of Cadbury's Roses. I will never forget that moment as both of us fought back tears of fulfilment. There are trophies that money can't buy.

26

Ghosts from the Past

The Leitrim Association in London invited me to attend a celebration function in the Galtymore ballroom on 29 February 2008. I was delighted as it would give me an opportunity to see London again. The members of Leitrim ladies intermediate football team were also guests as they had won the all-Ireland final the previous year. Among the other guests were: Damian Brennan, chairperson of Leitrim County Council; Myra Reynolds, editor of the *Leitrim Guardian*; John Gormley of Luton (formerly Cloone), president of the Leitrim London GAA; and David John Cooney, the Irish ambassador to London.

The invitation was for me and my carer, so Joe McGrath and I arrived in London the day before the dinner. Joe and I became friends in 1990. We met in Lourdes and he took care of me on many occasions. He was a lieutenant colonel in the Irish army and took part in UN peacekeeping activities in many countries but he always kept in touch with me by email or letter and a great friendship was born.

We left Dublin Airport with Ryanair on a cold stormy afternoon. Most of the lady footballers were on the same flight, as well as other people going to the function. From Luton, we took the train to Cricklewood. This had once been a familiar route for me. When we got off the train at Cricklewood, some of our young passengers were in a great hurry to get to the Crown Hotel. They turned left on approaching Cricklewood Lane, although I had advised them to turn right. What would an old fogey like me know about London? So I didn't say any more but my carer and I were the first to turn right. We proceeded the quarter of a mile to Cricklewood Broadway until I heard a voice saying, 'Follow Andy,' when the other group realised its mistake. I was like the Pied Piper of Hamelin leading this gang of about forty people to Cricklewood Broadway.

When we reached the Crown, I stood for a few seconds and looked at it, recognising each paving flag beneath my feet. I was standing where I had worked as a part-time barman for many years. I was on a high. This was the London I had said goodbye to forty-four years previously, never to return. The building hadn't changed a bit, because it's protected under conservation law, but on one side a new hotel has been erected. Moran's Crown Hotel is the proper name of the hotel where the association had booked accommodation for us. It's a beautiful circular structure with a lot of glass.

In the reception area, four receptionists were checking our group in. Joe approached the desk and enquired for my room, explaining that he was my carer. The receptionist said our room was on the second floor and asked, 'Is Andy with you?', as a fax had just arrived for me. When Joe read out the contents, what a surprise I got! It was from a friend who had anticipated my delight at being back in London again. Dated 29 February 2008, it read: 'Congratulations on your wonderful achievement: guest of honour at Leitrim Association dance. Your own people honouring you – it does not get much better than that. You have certainly earned for yourself this wonderful occasion. Savour the moment and enjoy.'

A poem followed, called 'The Great Panther – Andy'

> *The great panther returns once more,*
> *To pastures hunted many years before.*
> *All around Broadway he will look,*
> *As he tries to find an ancient nook.*
>
> *Old Father Time has done his job well,*
> *Matured now with so many tales to tell.*
> *On the Galty's floorboards he will tread,*
> *To stir up feelings he thought were dead.*
>
> *Tonight, in Galty, he will be the special guest,*
> *An honour, an opportunity, to shine his best.*

Leitrim people, how they hold him with pride,
Filled with happiness to have him by their side.

Tonight he will stand to address the crowd,
Deep within he surely will feel oh so proud.
Another of Ireland's sons, turned out so well,
A brave man with an incredible story to tell.

Andy, enjoy your trip down memory lane,
As you walk with the ghosts from the past again.
Have pride in your heart, as you take to your feet,
You have truly earned for yourself tonight's seat.

I was very moved by the poem. I knew this friend well but I was surprised by this ability to capture my feelings and present them so well in verse.

That night Joe and I went to the lounge in the old Crown bar. As usual there was a large crowd present, mostly people from Leitrim or with a Leitrim connection who had assembled for the following night's dinner dance. It was great to be back in London again.

After breakfast the next morning, we went for a stroll around town, to explore my old haunts and houses where I had lived in rented accommodation. I thought I might find some people I knew but, alas, some had died and the others had moved on. Cricklewood was a different place, with very few Irish in comparison with the 1950s. We returned to Broadway and spotted a public house with the name 'McGovern's' over the door. My friend Joe ordered drinks there. Austin, the young man running the premises, was a son of Peter McGovern, one of the people I took to London in 1955. He is a photocopy of his father, all energy and alertness and fully in control, regardless of how many people might be in the bar.

Joe went to pay for the drink but this young man, who had never seen us before, pushed the money back, saying, 'This one is on me.' Later, when he got a chance, he came out from behind the counter to greet me. He knew I was a guest at the Leitrim dinner dance. We talked about his deceased father. Peter McGovern was the proprietor of the Crown for many years and one of the most popular Irishman who ever descended on London. We had a few more drinks and young Austin insisted that everything was on him.

Back in Moran's we had dinner. I was tired and went to bed for a rest, knowing there was a long night before me. That afternoon we assembled in the lounge of the Crown. My daughter Sheila had travelled down from Scotland to be with me, and friends from the Tara football team of the 1950s joined us: Proinnsias (Francis) Redahan, Michael Gallagher from Mohill. James McGovern, the man I went to London with in 1954, and his wife, Peggy, were also there. Frank Keegan, chairperson of the Leitrim London Association, introduced me to the Irish ambassador, David Cooney, and his wife, Geraldine. Sean Faughnan, another committee member, was by my side, busy introducing me to people and assisting me in every way possible. The place was electric as Leitrim people poured in and the drink poured down. The committee had to work hard to get the people to leave the Crown, as dinner was about to begin in the Galtymore, a few hundred yards away.

When we entered, the place was a sight to behold. There were tables and chairs to accommodate five hundred people and a top table for guests and committee members. The principal guests were the footballers, as winning an all-Ireland at any level is something to be celebrated in Leitrim. I felt great pride at being included in the guest list, given that I had done nothing for Leitrim/London people except represent the disabled.

The Irish ambassador said he admired the courage of Leitrim people who had to emigrate to seek a living and make something of themselves in the 1940s, 1950s and 1960s. He also spoke of the courage of a Leitrim man with motor neurone disease with whom he had drinks earlier in the afternoon. All the guests received trophies and I was presented with an engraved silver plate for my work with disabled people and to honour the part I played in London in the 1950s and 1960s. In addition I received a cheque for £500 for the Association of People with Disabilities at home in Mohill. It was one of the proudest moments of my life.

This was how the association introduced me: 'Andy McGovern

was born in Aughavas in 1933. Andy came to London in 1954 and worked on the buildings and also as a barman in the famous Crown. In 1966, Andy and his wife, Bridgie, who married in St Agnes's Church in Cricklewood in 1961, returned to Ireland, where Andy set up his own machinery contracting business. In 1977, at the age of forty-three and with six children, he was diagnosed with the terminal illness known as motor neurone disease and was told his life expectancy was two to five years. Although there appeared to be no future Andy has amazed the medical profession for the past thirty-one years, although his hands and arms are virtually useless. He has written a book and has devoted his time to helping and encouraging other disabled people. He is a man with a great outlook and his courage and happiness spread to all who know him. He is a founder member of the Leitrim Association of People with Disabilities and is currently the association's PRO and a board member.'

We spent the next day wandering around London, having drinks in our old haunts. We had dinner in Kilburn with my daughter, Sheila, and her friend, Fiona, and again spent the night in the Crown. The next morning we were up early to begin our journey home.

I didn't feel in any way lonely leaving London. It was a different London from the 1960s, crowded with many different nationalities, and Cricklewood was not the same. This time I felt glad to leave, as it was no place for an old man. As the Ryanair aeroplane rose into the Luton sky, I smiled down at the landscape. I said to my friend Joe that I had carried the hod down there fifty years earlier and got no trophy; all I got was a sore shoulder. But I loved every minute of it.

The famous Galtymore ballroom opened its doors not long before I came to London in 1954. Two months after my return to London, in April 2008, it closed its doors for ever. Like many Irish people of that era, I arrived in London with a big empty suitcase and empty pockets. After I secured a job in a factory my first night out was in the Galtymore and I danced there twice a week for ten years, until I returned to Ireland in the mid-1960s.

27

A Hip Replacement against the Odds

I was seventy-eight in 2011 and finding my life very rewarding, despite my disability. I really enjoyed being part of a family, especially seeing my grandchildren growing up. Not having the use of my arms and hands did not bother me in any way. I just wondered how long this great life would last. One morning in October, I was out for my usual three-mile walk with the dog. I love this morning walk, when I breathe in the fresh, unpolluted air. The boreen I walk is narrow with some closed-in hedges and a strip of grass in the centre, indicating how little traffic there is on it.

I walk this route briskly, sometimes chatting to neighbours attending to their farming chores, such as Mike Joe Clancy and his son Michael. We exchange a joke and discuss the local gossip and, of course, the weather. I continue on by Francie Joe Quinn's and Jimmy Mulligan's. Jimmy might be out attending to his lawn, trees and shrubs and we have another interesting conversation with plenty of fun.

I move on to a much wider road, on which a few cars pass by and hoot. Some slow down to offer a lift but on seeing the dog they move on again. I use the dog as an excuse to continue my walk, as nobody wants to carry dog and man. Soon I reach Gubb's Cross, a landmark in the parish of Cloone about four hundred feet above sea level and somewhat isolated. From here I can look into five other counties: Cavan, Fermanagh, Sligo, Roscommon and Longford. What a view – and it's all free. I start my last lap home, energised by all this. Mickey Nicholls passes by in his purple jeep, with a big smile and another hoot.

This particular morning I had almost completed my circuit and turned into the narrow boreen once more, when I got a severe pain in my right groin, close to the hip. It interrupted my walk but as I was on an isolated boreen that very few people use, I knew I just had to grin and bear it. After a while, the dog, who had gone at least fifty yards ahead, came back and stood in front of me as if to say, 'What's up with you?' I found myself talking to the dog, saying, 'I'll be with you in a few minutes.' The pain eased a little and I started walking at a much slower pace. The dog ran on and stopped and looked back, knowing there was something amiss, The pain eased somewhat after I returned home but next morning it was there again, not too severe but always ready to erupt.

I consulted my GP, Arthur Dolan of Mohill, who prescribed some anti-inflammatory tablets. When I took one I felt that, if there were such a thing as being catapulted into Tír na nÓg, this must be it. I was back to my twenties; I could fly without wings. I had no pain whatsoever and when we went walking the following morning the dog was finding it hard to keep out of my way. I couldn't believe this improvement. After a few days, the pain returned but at least I knew that I had the answer and that another tablet would buy me some time.

Soon I discovered that I had to take a tablet every day. I told my friend, Val Fitzpatrick, who had had a hip replacement a few years previously, about my predicament. He said I would eventually have to have a hip replacement as I couldn't hold a stick or any balancing equipment because of my disability. He warned me that if my hip continued to worsen I would be in a wheelchair. I asked him if the anti-inflammatory tablets would control my arthritis. He pondered for a moment, then said, 'Yes they will put out the blaze but not the fire.' How true.

I returned to my GP and he increased the dose of tablets to two per day and sent me to Longford for an x-ray. Two weeks later I got the results, which showed severe osteoarthritis in my right hip. Again I sought my GP's advice. Was it possible for someone with MND to have a hip replacement? He said it was possible as long as the MND was not in my legs and immediately started to dictate a letter to Kieran O'Rourke, orthopaedic surgeon at St Vincent's Hospital, singing my praises and explaining that I was the longest

MND survivor in Ireland – thirty-five years by then. He added that I originally came from Aughavas, the same parish as Mr O'Rourke.

As the weeks went by the pain got worse, especially when I was trying to sleep. In January 2012 I received confirmation of an appointment for Mr O'Rourke's outpatients' clinic in St Vincent's. Mary, my daughter-in-law, came with me and I brought along the CD with the x-ray taken in Longford. Mr O'Rourke looked at it and asked me what I wanted him to do. I said that I would like to have a hip replacement. He smiled and said, 'Andy, I have no problem with replacing your hip but you have had motor neurone disease for the past thirty-five years and I would be very worried in case I disturbed this disease and make life worse for you. I also have my own reputation to protect.' I said I fully understood the situation but that if the arthritis continued I would be going into a wheelchair anyway. He agreed and said, 'I admire your courage.'

For a few minutes there was silence and then he said he would get in touch with my neurologist, Michael Hutchinson, who was still working at the same hospital, as well as an anaesthetist colleague, and if these two medical professionals declared me fit for an operation, he would do my hip replacement. I would be admitted to hospital for two days of tests and, if all went according to plan, he would do the operation without my having to go home again.

Two months later, in March 2012, I got a call to say there was a bed waiting for me in St Laurence's Ward in St Vincent's. When I arrived the nurse said I had a busy day ahead of me the next day with a lot of tests and, all going well, I was down for the hip operation two days later. I said goodbye to my son and daughter-in-law, who had brought me to Dublin, and assured them that I would be okay. We are not a family that expresses our emotions openly but the bond of love between us is very strong.

The next morning there was great activity, with nurses and medical staff around my bed. I had to have blood tests and a chest x-ray, also a hip x-ray and an ECG. Then I had to go for a pulmonary test to determine my respiratory function and breathing capacity for the anaesthetic. The woman who carried out this test checked my weight and height and asked my age. She inputted these into the computer and a diagram with some lines on it came from the printer. She told me that my respiratory and lung function would have to reach this standard, although there might be room for a little leeway. She inserted a mouthpiece and obstructed my nostril breathing, telling me to breathe in and fill my lungs to capacity, hold my breath, then breathe out and empty my lungs.

I did this a few times and she said, 'My God, I can't believe it. We will have to do this again. Take a rest for a few minutes.' Then I started again. Smiling, she said, 'You have far surpassed the required standard. I will get this result to your surgeon and your anaesthetist. I can assure you that there will be no problem with your having an anaesthetic, be it local or general. There is no trace of muscle wasting in your respiratory apparatus as a result of motor neurone disease. Your result would put some young people to shame.'

I was on a high when I heard this news. Hip replacement or no hip replacement, it meant I still had some living to do. That afternoon, Mr O'Rourke came to visit me. He said he had looked over my test results and that they were excellent. My neurologist, Professor Hutchinson, had also given the okay for my hip replacement.

The next morning, 22 March 2012, I was wheeled to the operating theatre, totally relaxed, as the previous day's tests had indicated that I was a healthy man. A woman who was a member of the anaesthetics team approached me after looking at my file.

'Andrew,' she asked, 'Could you tell me to what you attribute your survival with this terminal disease?' 'God and our Lady of Lourdes,' was my answer. She continued, 'I knew you were a miracle man. Can I touch you?' She rubbed her hands to my face and said, 'I have no doubt you received a miracle.'

I replied, 'I hope it continues.' I said an act of contrition and was at peace with myself, in no way frightened.

In the operating theatre, I was lifted on to a timber frame. Many members of medical staff were around me and Mr O'Rourke spoke to me but I got it hard to recognise him with his plastic cap. 'Andrew,' he said, 'You're making history today. You're the first person with motor neurone disease ever to have a hip replacement.' I replied that he must also be making history as first surgeon ever to

Three of Ireland's longest MND survivors: Mary Rice, Dublin (twenty-two years); and Jerry Leahy, Dublin (thirty-two years), with Andy at the AGM of the IMNDA in the Radisson Blu Hotel, Dublin, 2010.

replace a hip on a motor neurone patient.

Smiling, he instructed, 'Put this man to sleep.' Someone attached an oxygen mask to my face and others were trying to find a suitable vein in my arm. I looked at the clock and it was eleven. That was the last I remembered until I awoke in the recovery room. Someone was trying to remove the oxygen mask from my face but it seemed to be taped on and was hard to remove. Because of the anaesthetic I was bit aggressive and shouted at the man who was doing the job, 'Will you take the effing thing off!' The man smiled at me and said, 'Andrew, calm down, your operation is over and it was a success. You'll be back in your own ward soon.' I apologised for my outburst but he said this kind of thing was a common occurrence after an anaesthetic and that he had witnessed a lot worse.

After looking around me for a while, I spotted a clock and saw that it was five in the afternoon. Six hours of my life had passed that I knew nothing about. The operation was over and there was only one way from now on – up! Back in the ward, lying there in bed, I felt useless. I could barely move my legs and my arms were useless anyway. The nursing staff were all around me. I was treated like a baby, as everything had to be done for me. They offered me a meal that I refused, as I knew if I ate I would get sick. I took some tea and toast later on.

That night, I didn't sleep very well. I had tubes inserted in many places and I was in pain. The nurse give me some painkillers. The next morning two physiotherapists arrived and insisted on taking me out for a walk. They had a walking aid that reached to my chest and resting on it took some of the weight off my operated hip. I struggled with very short steps while one of the physiotherapists moved the frame. I went about five yards and had to call for a drink of water as I felt faint. They put me back into bed and told me I had done well but I knew that it was a poor display. When Mr O'Rourke came he told me that the operation had been a success but that it would take six or seven weeks before I walked properly again, that because I couldn't use any balancing equipment my recovery period would be longer than normal. After a week in hospital I would be moved to a care centre that specialised in physiotherapy.

The next morning, one of the physiotherapists arrived again with the walking frame. This time I went further and she praised me but I felt I did not deserve this praise. After she left, I sat there not able to move, watching elderly, frail women walking in the corridor with aids and sticks. I envied them, as in comparison with me they were moving at the speed of light.

On the third morning the physiotherapist brought a much smaller walking aid and we went about fifty yards down the corridor and back. With the help of a care assistant, she lifted me up and down in the chair a few times. I found my survival instinct kicking in. Although the flesh was weak, the spirit was strong. The next morning after breakfast, there was no one around and I had a great urge to stand up on my own. I knew that if I fell I would fall back into the chair so I stood and sat a few times and it was a wonderful boost to my confidence. The physiotherapist arrived and we went for another walk. Each session with the physiotherapist lasted only five or ten minutes as these professionals were in great demand and short supply in the hospital. This time I needed no praise as I knew I had turned the corner to improvement.

On the sixth day the two physiotherapists arrived and said I should try walking without the frame, with one on each side of me to catch me if I was in danger of falling. I walked a shorter distance with very little help. Back in the ward I practised movements the physios had shown me and I could walk the corridor with one physio.

Ten days after my operation. I went for a walk of a hundred yards or more with the physio, balancing myself independently. On our way back, we saw Mr O'Rourke and his team coming out of another ward. When he noticed me, Mr O'Rourke said he was impressed by my progress. I thanked him but said I still had a long way to go. But his secretary came to visit me that afternoon and said they were all astonished by how well I was doing and that they were going to send me to a care centre in Tallaght, where I would stay until I was fit to go home. Although Mr O'Rourke had mentioned this immediately after my operation I was a bit cast down by the sudden decision but I fully trusted the medical team. I had made many friends among the patients in the ward as well as with nurses and care personnel. One young fellow patient, Brian McCarroll, helped me by activating my mobile numbers Then he would hold the phone to my ear for me to make the call. Small things like that make such a difference.

That evening a taxi brought me to Kiltipper Woods, situated in the foothills of the Dublin Mountains. A physio came to tell me that she had plenty of work lined up for me the following morning. It was a state-of-the-art nursing home and everyone had their own room with TV, phone and shower and toilet. I was told to ring the bell if I needed anything but this was one thing I couldn't do so they gave me a room right beside the nurses' station and told me to say, 'Help!' instead.

I really enjoyed my stay at this centre and soon I was on first-name terms with most of the staff, who were of many nationalities. I didn't need any visitors, although a few came from Leitrim to see me, along with my family. The food was excellent, with a choice of menus. The staff encouraged the patients to interact, with most going to the dining hall for their meals, and there was plenty of entertainment in the form of films, sing-songs, dancing and cards.

Brian McCarroll, my new friend from St Vincent's, came to see me one day. I really appreciated his visit and found that the age gap between us did not matter at all. My communication with my children and grandchildren was a great asset to me and I could talk to any young person on any subject. We still keep in contact by email.

In the care centre, I concentrated on doing my physiotherapy in the physio workshop and getting my physical health back to what it had been. Finally, the physiotherapist said to me, 'Andy, I can't do much more for you. Would you like to go home? You can practise these movements in your own environment.' She said she could release me the next Friday. Like everyone else, I say I'm not superstitious but Friday the thirteenth did not appeal to me and there's also a superstition about Saturdays: 'Saturday's flitting has a short sitting.' So I suggested the Thursday afternoon and she agreed.

Andy, my son, and Mary, my daughter-in-law, came to collect me and I was sad to be leaving all the lovely people who had treated me so well over my ten-day stay, as well as the view of the Dublin Mountains. But inside I was on a high – home sweet home just three weeks after my operation and able to walk without aids or support to the waiting car. We arrived home at nine that evening and my twelve-year-old grandson had put the heat on in my house. It was like a dream come true. That night, as I lay in my own bed, I cried tears of joy. I must have thanked God a hundred times, as well as praying for all the staff in St Vincent's and Kiltipper Woods, who had helped me in my recovery. I had my hip replacement and no pain whatsoever. I had succeeded yet again, 'against the odds'.

28

How I Put In My Time

When I accepted my disease and disability, I found life interesting. People asked me how I put in my time, thinking that with no hands it must be awful. I have learned to deal with this and tell people who ask about my condition that my disability is only part of me.

To answer the question about how I put in my time: I started walking and enjoying the beauty of the countryside, something to which I had never paid much attention before. I took a particular interest in my grandchildren, who were living close by. They have never known me any other way but disabled but, in fact, they have never classed me as being disabled. At a very young age, they were eager to imitate my way of doing things. For example, before they could even talk, they were gesturing to their mother to let them have a straw in their cup. With my disability, I had started a trend. When they started going to primary school, I made it my business to meet them every day at the crossroads, a half-mile from home. I chatted to them and heard their little stories from school. One day I said to young Andy, 'You're getting very big. You're growing up and I'm growing down.' He answered immediately, 'No, Grandad, we are both growing up.' He didn't want to see this moment pass.

These conversations were priceless. I started naming for the children the different trees and plants in the hedgerows: the rowan, (mountain ash), the sally (willow) the whitethorn, the blackthorn, the ash, the sycamore, the fuchsia and the honeysuckle. I didn't have to consult any textbook or library as I knew these plants from my own rural upbringing. I showed them wild strawberries, telling them that they could eat them and that they were lovely. They really looked forward to this and ran on to find more and more, then back to me, sticking some of them into my mouth with their little fingers. I told them that when this crop was finished there would be raspberries and then there would be blackberries and that some day we would go to the bog and discover blueberries in the heather.

They asked me, 'Who put them here, Grandad?' I told them that God had created them, for primitive man's very survival depended on these fruit, berries and other earthly herbs millions of years ago. But now, man was so well off that he didn't need them any longer. I explained to them that all earthly species, be they animal, plant or human, depend on one another for survival. I told them that there were plenty of adults who did not realise why this fruit appeared every year, unnoticed and unwanted by so many. Were it not for my disability, I would never have taken the time to study this display of nature.

I found these wide-eyed children eager to meet me every day and ask more questions. I named for them every bird that flew past. I told them that when we were children, our favourite pastime in the spring was locating bird's nests and finding out how many eggs or young chicks were in them. We could never find out what was in one particular nest – the magpie's – as this nest was all thorns, impossible to get our hands into.

I found myself slowly being reunited with my forgotten child-hood. I learned so much by studying what was silently happening all around me with the changing seasons. I was sad to think of the farmers' enthusiasm to work their land in a manner that would produce more income, never once thinking of the environment, with their 10-10-20 fertiliser and their slurry.

During the school holidays, I took my grandchildren for walks in the countryside. These were much the same as the after-school variety, comprising questions and answers. I showed them the ruins of old houses where the occupants had moved away or died and explained how they had survived on a small piece of land with no tractor or car or any of today's equipment. I explained to them that some of these individuals had moved to foreign countries, dis-covered a better life and never returned.

One day, as we were walking in an isolated part of the country-side, there came a downpour of rain. Hurriedly we made our way to a clump of bushes and trees. I made an entrance and discovered a clear piece of ground, about four feet square, under a large tree, that sheltered us from the downpour. The children really enjoyed this hideaway. 'It's our little house, Grandad,' they said. We made many visits to this special place, even in good weather. The shrubs sprang back and concealed our path of entry and we could watch passing traffic, a tractor or a car, or even someone walking, but nobody could see us. It's amazing how the simplest of things can amuse children. This was their Disneyland and no Mickey Mouse could have made them happier.

I showed them the spot where my special flower appears every spring, a simple little primrose. I told them it always appears by the end of February or the beginning of March. I watch for the primrose every morning as I pass by and then one morning I find it has arrived. I celebrate inwardly when I see this apparition. I thank God that I have survived another year, still walking, and that this little flower has also survived the ravages of man with his hedge-cutting equipment and big machinery causing vibration in the ground where it lies unnoticed. I could find plenty of primroses far more decorative and tended to by experienced gardeners but this one was my favourite. I had been noting its appearance for the previous twenty years and its very survival never failed to amaze me. One day it would appear and I would not. I asked the children to promise me that when they returned home from their travels to faraway places they would look out for this little flower.

I got so much from the dancing eyes before me, more than I could ever get from an able-bodied life. At times I felt a great sense of regret. We had reared six beautiful children of our own but I had never discovered the magic of being with them during those pressured years. It was up to me to go out working and bring home the bacon. Bridgie was at home every day but she too had a lot of work to do and there was no time for walks and talks with the children. These magic years pass us by and can never be replaced. The best you can hope for is to get a second bite at the cherry, as I did with my grandchildren. My disability had provided this wonderful benefit.

My favourite season is spring. During my young, able-bodied life,

I always looked forward to the spring, the start of the new farming year, the ploughing, sowing and planting of the crops, the turning over of a fresh sod of earth with its beautiful smell released into the atmosphere. One thing that always amazed me was that no sooner had the plough turned over the soil than the seagulls arrived from nowhere, making squawking, celebratory sounds. How they got the message I will never know. We live at least sixty miles from the coast and not one seagull was in sight until the sod was turned and the earthy aroma released. Seagulls then invaded the upturned sod and feasted on the worms, grubs and insects. Ploughing for crops here in Leitrim is a thing of the past but I believe that if it took place again, seagulls would return.

Now in my twilight zone and disabled, I have only a distant memory of the springs of my youth. I'm in no way saddened by this as I have a new interest in the springs of my disabled life. I look at the wonderful works of nature erupting all around me. I awoke this morning to the sound of birdsong, the morning chorus. I opened the bedroom window and lay for a few minutes more, taking in nature's indication that winter is over or at least on the way out. I was oblivious of such things during the years I was doing physical work.

After breakfast today, I went for my usual stroll, down a long 'boreen', or narrow country road. Spring was everywhere to be seen. The rejuvenation of shrub life was evident, with buds on the white-thorn, sycamore and currant bush. Bluebells, daffodils, dandelions, daisies and primroses replaced snowdrops. Frogs were spawning in the water holes, while a few newborn lambs played in a field nearby. Rabbits popped up and down in the distance and pheasants cackled. The musical sound of swans flying past alerted me to look up. They were on their way to search for new water for the breeding season. They too knew that spring had arrived.

I walked for about two miles into quiet, almost forgotten terri-tory: pure, unspoiled beauty, with not a car in sight. The nearest exhaust pipe was in an aeroplane, flying high in the sky. I chose a flagstone on a nice, mossy bank and sat down. Here I spent some time in total solitude, taking in good, clean, fresh air. I closed my eyes and relaxed completely. An ass brayed in the distance, hens cackled at a neighbour's house and the cock responded – all sounds that are fast becoming obsolete. This is heaven, my heaven, reminding me that I am the child of a great God.

In my youth, I travelled away from Ireland, my eager heart demanding excitement and adventure, but now I'm happy to have found again my forgotten heritage and remain in my native habitat. Oliver Goldsmith expresses this desire in 'The Deserted Village':

> *And, as an hare whom hounds and horns pursue,*
> *Pants to the place from whence at first she flew,*
> *I still had hopes, my long vexations past,*
> *Here to return – and die at home at last.*

As I stood up I thanked God for giving me the intellect to witness the transformative power of new life. The cuckoo would arrive soon; the swallows would return from South America, without map or compass, and find their nests in the lofts and sheds of County Leitrim, Donegal, Cavan, Louth or Dublin – whichever location they had left the previous September. This cycle of new life recurs every spring and no scientist can stop it or make it happen. Yet some ignoramus will tell you, 'There's no such thing as a miracle.' I returned home with tingling sensations of adrenaline in the back of my neck and a spring in my step.

I have witnessed more springs than I can remember. But it is only now that I am disabled that I really appreciate this recurring resurrection. Today I am a happy person. I may have been dealt a severe blow but I have an awful lot to live for. In the words of Richard Bach in *Jonathan Livingston Seagull*: 'Break the chains of your thought, and you break the chains of your body, too.'

Because MND didn't prove fatal to me in the prognostic estimate of three to five years, I was given the opportunity to look at my life in a new way. My disease is no longer in control of me; quite the contrary. I mingle with the disabled and the able-bodied. I can look the able-bodied in the eye and know that I'm as good as them. I had the thought that they eat, drink, talk and walk too quickly. But on reflection, I realised I was making an unfair judgement as they are entitled to eat, drink, walk, run and act at whatever speed their body and mind allow. They have a right to this freedom. I once did all the things they do with ease and speed and I too have the right to do these things at my own reduced speed and level of output.

It's hard enough. I want people to have patience with me, to understand when I drink through a straw, when I struggle to shake hands awkwardly, when I fail to open doors and when I ask for assistance: to bear with my inadequacy because of my debilitating disease. I want all these things from able-bodied people but I need to have the same expectations of myself; to be patient with myself, to wait and, in my waiting, learn to accept my status in life as a disabled person growing in dependency on my able-bodied friends. That's the hard part.

I begin to list my own abilities, beginning with 'I can' or 'I am able to'. For example, I can listen to another person's story, to music, to birdsong. I can smile to brighten someone's day. I can laugh. I can think. I can write. I can read. I can drink Guinness through a straw – it tastes the same. I can enjoy fun. I can love. The list is endless. I invite you, my able-bodied friend, to list your own abilities and give thanks too, particularly for all the little things you take for granted.

Andy and Bridgie McGovern with their children at the wedding of their daughter, Pauline, in August 2006. From left: Anita, Andrew, Sheila, Andy, Pauline, Pauline's husband, Ryan Cremins, Bridgie, Raymond and Caroline. (Photo: Shawn Degnan)

Epilogue

Now in my twilight years, my heart easy and mind at rest, I think back to where it all started. I think of that little boy trying to follow his father through a freshly ploughed field. The father is in the company of his faithful friend, the old horse, and when the plough-ing is complete he ties the horse securely at the headland. Now the father casts oat seeds from a bucket and the child wonders why he is throwing the beautiful, golden seeds away. Nobody explained it to me but as the weeks and months went by, I watched growth transform the crop into different colours, finally a spectacular gold. Again, to my dismay, my father intervened. His scythe, along with those of his neighbours, reduced this golden sea of beauty to bundles of corn. Later it was taken to the haggard to be threshed.

As I watched the golden seeds fall into the hopper from the threshing mill, filling the bags, I learned fast without teacher or textbook. My father had not been throwing anything away when I struggled to follow him in the spring of 1937, but multiplying a hundredfold. Now he was reaping the harvest of his work. The precious grains would be turned into food for cattle and humans and only the best seeds were stored for the next year's crop. At this point I knew where my morning porridge came from and realised that the land was instrumental in our very survival.

It is amazing that sometimes a casual remark can be the spark that ignites something in a listener. Twenty-five years ago I was watching the *Late Late Show* one night. Gay Byrne was interviewing John Bowman, Brush Shields and Brendan Kennelly and they were discussing the subject of mortality and how best a person could ensure that their memory survived after they had departed this world. The guests all agreed on one thing: offspring, preferably a son, so that their name would be carried on to future generations.

Brendan Kennelly suggested that there were other ways by which an individual might make sure he was remembered. One was to plant a tree, which would outlive many generations. Another was to write a book that someone in the future would pick up and read.

That night I pondered the interview. I had offspring: two sons and four daughters. I had planted many trees in my time, not in order to be remembered but for the sheer comfort of the shelter. We live on a hilltop and although we are blessed with a scenic view, some of the storms we experienced were frightening and caused structural damage. So for me planting some trees was a necessity, not a memorial. I felt sad to think that Brendan Kennelly's other recommendation – writing a book – was something far beyond my ability. I had only primary school education and my disability meant that picking up a pen had become a thing of the past. I could not use a typewriter, keyboard or any other method of processing text. At this time, computers were only for specialists.

As the years went by my yearning to write kept nagging at me as I was aware that there was a mountain of information held captive in my active mind. Being able to write my name with a foot-controlled mouse was the seed of all my future writing achievements. At last the imprisoned thoughts could be released.

I wrote this memoir with today's voice recognition software. It may not be a bestseller but this does not worry me. It's my book and I have done it my way. I have achieved Brendan Kennelly's three types of lasting memorial. Thank God for remarks like his.

As I enter my eighty-first year, I look back on the harvests I lived through. I too reaped my rewards. I ploughed my own furrow and spent time standing forlorn on the headland. I experienced times in barren ground, struggling to survive, as well as the joys and fulfilment of reaching maturity. With a great sense of energy and vitality, I reached my peak but the hand of fate was to turn the tide, when, at forty-three, I received a diagnosis with a life expectancy of two to five years.

In the depths of despair, I struggled, as the disease gradually manifested itself. I was overwhelmed by a dark cloud. Floods of anger, bitterness and despair rained down on to my once happy life. I feared most for those I loved most and the vision of my wife and children tormented me at night. How would they manage without me? I asked God how this sentence could be handed down to me, a healthy man. The more I searched, the more frustrated I became, facing a wall of silence, not knowing that acceptance was the answer.

Today, as I remember those far-off days of despair, my heart is filled with emotions, but thank God they are different emotions. It is as if a power from above granted me my three wishes: health, wealth and happiness. In the early days of my diagnosis I could never have imagined how happily I now live in harmony with my disability and the good health I enjoy. I have wealth in abundance but I do not measure my wealth in material things but the priceless commodities money cannot buy. Gone are the worries about material things, replaced by a wonderful appreciation of all I have.

I am contented with my lot. I appreciate my restful night's sleep in my modest Leitrim home. I awaken and rejoice with the birds in the morning. Anchored as I am in nature, I share their songs of happiness. I look on each day as God's treasure, given to me to enjoy. I have a good sense of humour and please God it will always stay with me. I have long since left my zone of self-pity and being like a helpless victim. I feel I am a lucky human being who happened to have MND as part of my experience of life. My life is full of confidence and purpose. My disease changed my life completely, enriching my humanity. I live my life at a slower pace and I can take time to enjoy it thoroughly. I savour each precious moment. I can relax and listen to the silence, which has so much to say.

My wife, Bridgie, is now in a nursing home in Mohill. Although it was necessary for her to move there in order to receive the best possible care, it was a heart-wrenching separation and her absence created an enormous vacuum in my life. However, my family and grandchildren come more often to visit, something that has helped to banish the silence. We are still together in spirit and I visit her frequently. I thank God we still have each other and that both of us are enjoying reasonably good health.

My six energetic children, in whom I have such pride, are all living their own lives. My four daughters are abroad but with modern technology they remain very close and are always in my heart. No distance can weaken the bond between parent and children. My two sons live close by and are always available when I need a little chore to be done. Their love and devotion are what sustain me and allow me to live independently. Each of my grand-children means the world to me. I am proud to see my own reflections in their developing personalities, especially the wit and humour handed down from past generations. They are the ones who keep me 'forever young'. My sister Rosaleen died twenty years ago but my brother, Jack, lives in the home place, Corroneary. We meet up for a drink every week and he is always willing to make himself and his car available to me.

I have a very special relationship with my daughter-in-law, Mary, who is my personal carer. As with all my family, the words of love that are engraved in my heart could never adequately be transferred to paper but I know that my feelings will live on in their hearts after I am gone. My home helps are magnificent and no task is a problem to them as, together, we greet each day with humour and laughter. I have many friends, all of whom make their own lovely contribution to my life, and I treasure them.

I thank God for being in this blessed spot and pray that he will leave me here for just another day to savour the wonderful view. The poet William Ernest Henley, who had more than his share of health troubles, put it better than I can in his poem 'Invictus' (1875):

> *Beyond this place of wrath and tears*
> *Looms but the horror of the shade,*
> *And yet the menace of the years*
> *Finds, and shall find me unafraid.*

> *It matters not how strait the gate,*
> *How charged with punishments the scroll.*
> *I am the master of my fate:*
> *I am the captain of my soul.*